Stephanie's Emerald Fever

L.J. Maxie

Topaz Publishing

L.J. Maxie

Stephanie's Emerald Fever

L. J. Maxie

All Rights reserved.

Copyright © May 2010 L.J. Maxie

Cover Art Copyright © July 2011 Dawné Dominique,

Topaz Publishing

This is a work of fiction. All characters and events portrayed in this novel are fictitious or used fictitiously. All rights reserved, including the right to reproduce this book, or portions thereof, in any form.

Publisher:

Topaz Publishing

topazpublishing@aol.com

www.ljmaxie.webs.com

Stephanie's Emerald Fever

Dedicated to the Son of the Living God
Stephanie's Emerald Fever is in your hands
Leviticus 25:21

In Loving Memory
Beloved Mother
Voncil Wallace, who journeyed home during the last revision of SEF

Dedication
My Husband, Arlistel, the love of my life, and the real Uncle June Bug

My Dad, O. D. Wallace, for giving me a wonderful sense of humor

Acknowledgements
Marilyn Godfrey, my partner in crime

Aworuwa Bosede, Yoruba Translations

L.J. Maxie

Preface

As a little girl, there was no other place I'd rather be than seated at the feet of my Grandmother. When resting from her labor, Grandmother would quietly rock back and forth, soaking up God's pure sunlight. She didn't talk very much, so when she did speak, I listened. Grandmother was born at the turn of the century. Her Papa told her about life in slavery and she, in turn, told us. Those stories became invaluable to our family.

Grandmother also told us stories about 'Green Plum Fever,' an illness contracted from eating an abundance of yellowish-green plums. This fever caused hallucinations that were not distinguishable from real life. Often these hallucinations guided the fevered mind on a life-changing journey. In "Stephanie's Emerald Fever" Stephanie learned that walking in a person's shoes can actually foster understanding. Stephanie's Emerald Fever has the potential to unite people from various backgrounds. It supports a cause that cuts across superficial boundaries and promotes tolerance.

Stephanie's Emerald Fever

Introduction

Sixteen-year-old Stephanie Andrews takes for granted the people who love her most. Her snobbish attitude and stubborn ways create big trouble with the family's housekeeper, Madge. Madge's history with the Andrews family extends as far back as the early 1800s. Having raised Stephen Andrews, Stephanie's father, Madge is an honorary member of the Andrews family. Hailing from a long line of slaves on the Andrews' plantation, Madge knows that being Black is not as easy as Stephanie thinks. Her attempts to elicit respect from Stephanie are lost. However, Stephanie is impatient with Elderly Madge and scoffs at her family's history.

While on an outing with friends, Miss Andrews, a courageous sampler of new cuisines, tries an irresistible and rare green plum dressing. From this daring feat, she develops a highly unusual case of food poisoning. The resulting fever that engulfs Stephanie's body hurls her into an imaginary but realistic life-changing adventure.

"Stephanie's Emerald Fever" is not your average story of cruel deeds, penance, and salvation. The journey that Stephanie Andrews embarks upon is so much more. With characters ranging from dainty southern women to scrappy, scraggly slaves, "Stephanie's Emerald Fever" will increase understanding, tearing down barriers between the past and the present.

So, journey with Stephanie Andrews as she is harshly separated from her shallow box of reality and forced to experience life as a slave on her own family's plantation. Humorous circumstances and mind-boggling events rupture her steel-like exterior, exposing the compassion within. The fever will weave you in and out of Stephanie's tempestuous adventures then land you safely home. Do you have the stamina to withstand "Stephanie's Emerald Fever?"

Stephanie's Emerald Fever

Contents

Acknowledgements

Preface

Introduction..Page

1	Who Died And Made You Queen?...............9	
2	Selfish, Spoiled and Disrespectful...........22	
3	An Elaborate Set-..................................37	
4	What is This Place?........................56	
5	I Don't do Windows............................68	
6	What Happened to my Beautiful Voice?...79	
7	You ain't nuttin' special 'round here!........93	
8	But, I Love Shopping........................104	
9	Whew! What is That Smell?....................117	
10	Oh, my Aching Legs!...........................137	
11	A Painful Past....................................143	
12	Is There Freedom in Shrimp Gumbo?......172	
13	I've Been in Your Skin 187	
14	A Long Journey to Nowhere...............200	
15	When Did I Become a Witch?................213	

Yoruba Translation of Phrases.....................236

Chapter One

Who Died and Made You Queen?

"You infuriating piece of fat trash!"

Stephanie's Emerald Fever

The mall is excellent hunting ground when scouting for hot guys and cool clothes. Nevertheless, the entire stalking experience can be totally overwhelming. So, when the chase is over, dinner with friends is the best way to relax. That is, unless you're surrounded by insensitive juveniles who volunteer your precious services for a high school fundraiser!

Stephanie's cat-like eyes sparked with blue fire. How dare Brittany volunteer her valuable energy to chair a dull old fundraiser? Staring directly into Brittany's timid eyes, Stephanie gathered her blonde hair into a bundle, untangled it, then violently tossed it behind her small shoulders.

"Really Brittany!" Stephanie blasted. "Really. I swear you are the most annoying creature I know." She drummed her fingers impatiently on the table. "How could you like, assume I wanted to chair that stuffy old fundraiser?" Turning her oval face from Brittany's view, she sulked. "Irritating!"

Though Brittany was one of Stephanie's most loyal friends, she was a bit intimidated by Stephanie's self-absorbed attitude. After an eleven-year friendship, Brittany knew Stephanie had a temper like a wild bull. Dodging the raging shower of horrible insults, Brittany constricted her almond shaped eyes. She toyed nervously with her reddish brown hair which lay about her shoulders. While she waited for the hail of fire to cease, she gathered the courage to speak.

"But, Stephanie. You did say the last fundraiser was lame. You said you could do a better job in your sleep. So, when Mrs. Russell asked for my nomination, I threw your name in the hat." She shrugged innocently. "Come on. It'll be fun."

Despite the fact that Stephanie's cherubim lips were the envy of every girl at school, caustic words spewed from them easily. "You infuriating piece of fat trash! You knew I was only trying to make Allison look incompetent. I couldn't let on that her fundraiser was awesome."

Looking downward, Brittany inspected the small pudge in her stomach. "I'm not fat!" She winced. "Am I? Honestly, you can be so mean." Turning toward Nancy for agreement, Brittany's plea was met with intentional silence.

Nancy pretended to brush lint from her short skirt. "Huh?" she asked, looking awkwardly at Brittany. "I'm sorry. I didn't hear you." As Nancy smoothed her skirt, her hazel eyes assured, "I told you she'd be ticked."

"Darn right I'm ticked," Stephanie sassed. She reached for her menu. Raising a brow, she scrutinized Nancy's new hair style. "Nan," she crooned spitefully. "I meant to ask you earlier. Did your little brother cut your hair with the hedge trimmers?" A devilish smiled played across her lips. "Oh! And, brunette." She shook her head sadly. "Not your color."

Nancy grasped the wispy ends of her short hair, spiking them with her fingertips. Bashfully, she admitted, "This color might be wrong for me, but I happen to like my new haircut." Nancy placed her menu aside. "Now, people can see my new earrings."
With a placid expression, Stephanie stared into Nancy's eyes. "They aren't that great. Believe me."

From the corner of her eye Stephanie noticed a middle-aged server as she bounced energetically from the kitchen. Balancing three glasses of water, she rushed toward the table. "Good evening, my name is Margaret. I'll be your server this evening. Are you guys ready to order?"

"That depends, Margaret," Stephanie mocked. "Some of us just can't seem to think for ourselves." In a condescending tone Stephanie asked, "Do I need to order for you, Brittany? You want to make decisions for me. It's only fair that I make a few decisions for you."

Margaret was clearly shaken from her task. "Woah! Do you guys need to talk among yourselves?"

Brittany folded her tanned arms and sneered. "Stephanie!"

Stephanie twirled her wrist in a majestic manner and addressed the server. "Margaret, Brittany will have the potato skins and the Swiss burger." She mouthed the words, "Heavy on the onions."

Stunned, Brittany sat upright. "Onions! Hey! I don't want a Swiss burger." She cast her gaze toward Stephanie. "I do want the Chicken Salad Classic." Acknowledging Stephanie's hostile take-over, her full lips became a pout.

Nancy tried to comfort Brittany by patting her arm. Leaning toward her, she whispered, "Don't let Stephanie push your buttons." Pleasantly, she addressed the server. "Cucumber squares for me, please."

Stephanie turned toward the server and droned, "It's difficult when you're the only person in the group who has class. I'll have the Four Seasons Salad," she said promptly. "And, I'll have that with chicken, pecans, and mandarin oranges." She closed her menu. "Also, I'd like to try the house dressing." Completing her statement, she cocked her head to one side and gawked at her server.

Hesitantly, the server tapped her pencil against her pad. "Do you want the Green Plum Dressing?" Stephanie had never had Green Plum Dressing a day in her life, but she answered, "Of course."

"It's an acquired taste," Margaret warned. "Do you like tart dressings?"

Stephanie's Emerald Fever

Stephanie looked at the server as if she were a misshapen statue. "Whatever," she shunned, shooing Margaret away.

"O-kay," Margaret sighed. "I guess that'll be all." Puzzled, she walked away pushing her pencil behind her ear.

With a judgmental glare, Stephanie watched the server until the heavy kitchen doors closed behind her. She turned up her pointed nose. "Honestly, she was like, all in our business."

Nancy fished out her lemon and squeezed it into her water. After taking a small sip she asked, "What did she say?"

Scowling, Stephanie fumed. "It isn't *what* she said. It was that dumb look on her idiotic face." Preparing for the wait, Stephanie made herself comfortable on her padded seat. "Anyone could tell she was jealous of us. Hello! She works in a restaurant. What's that all about?"

"You really think she's jealous?" Nancy asked clicking her nails. "Maybe she has a family to support."

Reaching out, Stephanie placed her hand atop Nancy's to stop the noise. "Don't you know that's, like, irritating?"

Checking the activity behind her, Stephanie asked, "Did you see that gut?" She gently pressed her toned tummy in comparison. "Flab-by. I mean really, she must have a house full of piglets."

Being fed up with Stephanie's superior attitude, Brittany pursed her lips and looked away.

Nancy's hazel eyes surveyed the elegant sights of the restaurant. Quietly, she sipped her water.

Infuriated, Stephanie huffed, "Oh, come on! Admit it. She's a hopeless slob! Didn't you see that dried food on her apron? I mean, what's that all about?"

Brittany folded her arms and boldly informed Stephanie, "An apron is for catching food, Stephanie. You are wrong on so many levels."

"Rrrright," Stephanie growled, averting her eyes. She raised her own silken locks. "Now, you've got to admit, her hair is a rat's nest." Feeling as though she had a worthy discussion she added, "And oh my gosh—how thin can hair get before you declare it legally gone."

Brittany tried desperately to change the temperature at the table. "Her shoes were cool." She gazed at Nancy for support, but received none.

Stephanie became inflamed. "Her shoes? She probably got those things at the Bargain Basement—on the sidewalk-in the trash!" she snickered loudly. "Oh, speaking of hired help. Did you guys ever hire that new maid?"

Stephanie's Emerald Fever

Relieved that the conversation had taken a turn, Brittany wriggled contentedly on her seat. "Not yet. I know we'll never find one as great as Madge."

Stephanie flinched. "Garh, Madge is not our maid! Well, she was, but my dad, like adopted her or something." She picked up her silverware and checked for spots. "He just didn't want to put the old nag out to pasture. She's like, the oldest piece of furniture in the entire house."

Remembering Madge, Nancy smiled fondly. "But, she's such a sweetheart. She treats us better than our own parents."

"Rrrright," Stephanie groaned, averting her eyes.
Nancy gushed, "Although you're sixteen she always calls you things like Sweet Pea, and Sweetie Pie and stuff like, Snookums."

Covering their mouths, Nancy and Brittany tried desperately to stifle a pleasant giggle.

Stephanie displayed her upturned palm to halt the laughter. "Okay, you humor hounds. That's enough. I guess you guys find it amusing that I was raised by an old black woman."

A soft smile came to rest on Brittany's lips. "It doesn't matter what color she is, Stephanie. She's still a nice person."

Stephanie folded her arms "Like, we have a lot in common, right? Me and an old black woman. Give me a break. Besides, she's so old she can hardly walk." Exasperated, Stephanie threw up her hands. "She's like, almost a hundred!"

Disregarding Stephanie's terrible statement, Nancy piped up. "Wasn't she like, your Dad's nanny or something?"

Stephanie's eyes narrowed. "I think, I said we've finished talking about her." Although Stephanie was not finished talking about Madge, Nancy knew that statement was her egotistical way of changing the subject. "Anyway, Nan-cy. Didn't your doctor take your braces off way too soon?"

Instantly, Nancy's hand went to her mouth. "Why would you say that?"
Pointing at Nancy's mouth, Stephanie chuckled. "Because, you have lip gloss on your front teeth. Your teeth are kinda like, hugging each other."

"No way!" Nancy squalled, briskly rubbing her teeth.

Brittany hurled a frown at Stephanie. Sympathetically, she reached into her purse for a mirror. She gave the mirror to Nancy who was frantic with embarrassment. "Stephanie Andrews, you are simply wicked."

Stephanie arched a brow. "Thank you," she nodded majestically. "I try hard."

While Nancy calmed herself down, Brittany closed her eyes against Stephanie's childlike behavior.

Ignoring Brittany, Stephanie looked toward the kitchen. "When is that witch going to bring our food? It's like, taking her forever."

Brittany seethed quietly. "The server does not cook the food, Stephanie." Noticing their server's arrival she brightened. "Here she comes now." Pushing her silver aside, Brittany made room for her large plate.

Margaret placed her huge serving tray upon a stand. The food looked appetizing and smelled heavenly. "Okay girls. Let's see." She passed out the plates. "You had the cucumber squares. And you, the Chicken Salad Classic. And last but not least, the Four Seasons Salad with green plum dressing." Stephanie gawked at Margaret as she placed her plate before her. "It's about time. We were about to starve here."

"Thank you," Nancy said sweetly. "This looks great."

"I'm good," Brittany said waving her hand.

The server looked over the table. "Do you girls need anything else?"

"Do you need a hair appointment?" Stephanie sassed. She opened her mouth and stuck her finger inside as if she'd throw up."

The server froze as she observed Stephanie's behavior. Frowning, she shook her head. "I've dealt with some strange snobs, but you are the worst ever." Briskly removing the empty tray, she turned and walked away. "Enjoy your meal," she called.

"Yeah," Stephanie chuckled. "Go nurse your fat kids," she snickered.

Daintily, Nancy picked up her cucumber sandwich. "Stephanie that was really mean. She already thinks you're a snob."

Pouring the dressing over her salad, Stephanie jeered. "You say that like it's a bad thing."

Brittany eagerly took pleasure in her meal. She shook her fork at Stephanie. "I have my doubts about you, Stephanie. My family has like," she munched, "traveled all over the world. I've never see anyone so insensitive. I mean, you treat people so badly."

Stephanie gazed up at Brittany. "Oh, shut up! I'm only telling the truth. We're still going to Paris this summer, right?"

Brittany shook her head doubtfully. "Sure! We are. I just hope you learn how to treat people before then. You're like, so..." Looking around the room Brittany cringed. "...embarrassing."

Shaking an orange slice on the end of her fork, Stephanie confronted Brittany. "So, you don't like the way I talk to people. I just call it the way I see it."

Brittany informed, "Some thoughts should stay in your head, Stephanie." She swallowed. "It isn't cool to say everything on your mind."

"And who made that law?" Stephanie asked, pouring more dressing on her salad.

Nancy studied her plate intensely. "You hurt people's feelings," she whispered quietly.

Stephanie almost spit out her food. She pointed to herself. "Me! Really." She wiped her mouth on her napkin. "I'm only telling the truth. How can I hurt a person's feelings if I'm telling the truth? You think it! I say it!"

Brittany shook her head despondently. "You really have no idea, do you?"
Feeling under attack, Stephanie defended herself. "What is this, random statement day? You guys are way too sensitive." Stephanie pursed her lips. "One word from me and everyone runs for the tissue box." She took a large sip of water. "What's really going on?"

Brittany became antsy. "We aren't going back to the mall after we finish are we?"

Surprised, Stephanie shot back, "Sure, why not. I didn't finish shopping. We could go back to that little shop near the food court," she teased. Nancy held her nervous stomach. "We can't go back there! The manager called security once!" She whispered, "I was like, so scared. If you guys go back, I'm calling my mom to pick me up."

"Stephanie, you did go off on that manager. Didn't she Nan?" Brittany nodded knowingly.

Reaching for her check Stephanie declared, "You guys—I wasn't scared of that woman."

Brittany slowly finished her meal. "Let's go back to the arcade." Her voice lifted in a harmonizing tone. "I saw some really hot guys before we left."

Stephanie smiled. "Yeah, a delicious redhead in particular." Anxiously, the girls finished their meal, grabbed their packages, and rushed out of the restaurant. After a date with a *Scary Movie*, the girls hung around the arcade. Occasionally, the mating rituals of the male species earned a hearty giggle. Before they realized it, time had vanished.

Chapter Two

Spoiled, Selfish, And Disrespectful

"Skin like yours, like that'll happen!"

Chapter Two

After an evening of fun, Stephanie found herself standing in the corridor of their downtown apartment. Because her arms were crammed with shopping conquests, she found it difficult to get her key in the door.

Placing her knee against the door, she tried desperately to balance her purse as well as the slippery bags. Fidgeting, she managed to turn the key. Simultaneously, the intricately carved door swung open.

Stephanie's eyes searched the dimly lit room. It was late; she wondered if elderly Madge was asleep. Using her elbow, she pushed the wall switch. The room was filled with brilliant light. A clean scent of freshly polished furniture greeted her.

Snagging her heels in the plush carpet, Stephanie's keys slipped from her fingers and landed near her foot. "Just great!" With a scowl on her angelic face, she called, "Madge! Would you, like, *please* get these packages? I've dropped my keys!" Impatiently, Stephanie allowed the packages to slip from her grasp.

Stephanie's Emerald Fever

Using her wooden cane, Madge hobbled down the stairs. At last, she met Stephanie at the door. "I'm sorry, Sweet Pea, but I was trying to clean your closet and didn't hear you come in." She noticed the pile of crumpled packages on the floor and cringed. "You sure can spend your parents' money."

"I know, right," Stephanie giggled proudly.

Madge glimpsed the clock and noted the time. "I thought Brit's parents were going to drop you off before eleven."

"Well," Stephanie hesitated. "We were having so much fun the time just slipped away. Brit didn't call her parents until late."

Madge walked slowly toward the end table, placed her gnarled fingers under the lampshade and turned on the light. "I was trying to keep myself busy until you made it safely home."

She leaned her cane against a marble-top table near the door and turned off the lights beaming overhead. Reaching down to gather packages, Madge stopped short of her task. Reflecting signs of physical pain, a grimace disfigured her slender brown face.

Stephanie closed her eyes, shutting out the awful sight. Tossing her blonde hair over her shoulder, her smile turned sour. "Don't tell me your back is hurting again. Aren't you, like, tired of chewing on that same old complaint?" She shook her head in disgust. "Didn't dad tell you not to do anymore housework around here? After all, aren't you more like family?"

Madge looked as if she had been slapped and rewarded at the same time. Mixed emotions quickened her breath while her aging eyes followed Stephanie's exaggerated movements. "I know what your dad said, Sugar," she said stiffly. "Your mom and dad have always treated me like family."

Stephanie quipped, "I hope you aren't looking for sympathy."

Shrugging, Madge shook her head. "It's just hard to stop being a housekeeper. I know I'm getting on in age." Picking up one of the packages she looked at Stephanie. "Aren't you going to help, Sugar? Bending over hurts my old back."

Stephanie leered. "I don't think so."

Confused by Stephanie's unwillingness to help, Madge picked up another package and held it in her fist. "Have you forgotten I raised your father?"

Stephanie rolled her eyes toward the ceiling. "Like, I know you kept my dad. Garh! Heard it a million times!" Reaching down, Stephanie hastily loaded Madge's arms with packages that slid off and tumbled to the floor.

Selfishly, Stephanie stood up. "I really don't know why mom and dad keep you around. We've had a housekeeper for years."

Madge closed a torn package and twisted the top. "They are just good, decent people. They probably feel I have no place to go but to the rest home," Madge said humbly.

"But, aren't you, like, almost dearly departed?" Ignoring Madge's new dilemma, Stephanie walked past her and snatched up her keys. She hurled herself upon the posh sofa, pulling her cell phone out of her jacket. After checking her texts she placed it on the coffee table.

Kicking off her uncomfortable shoes, Stephanie admitted, "I really could use a soda, I'm totally parched. My lips are so dry they hurt." She ran her fingers across her chapped lips. With her leg tucked beneath her, she rummaged inside her purse for lip gloss. After sliding the wet substance across her cherubim lips, she pressed them together. Turning her attention toward Madge she asked, "How old are you, anyway? Almost a hundred?"

Madge was puzzled by Stephanie's offensive behavior. Restacking the packages, she sarcastically acknowledged Stephanie's help. "Thanks for the help with the packages, missy."

Stephanie closed her purse. "Sure anytime."

This time Madge rolled her eyes toward the ceiling. "To answer your question about my age, I'm almost eighty-five." In a forgiving manner she added, "Your dad told me to give you the same firm, but loving, hand I gave him."

Stephanie cast her hand aside and shot back. "Whatever!" Noticing that Stephanie had been unbearably rude all evening, Madge frowned. "Excuse me?" Her eyes followed Stephanie's rude hand gesture.

Pulling off her stylish pink jacket and tossing it across the sofa, Stephanie asked, "Is it hot in here or what?" She reached under the end table and pulled several tissues from a decorative tissue box. Blotting the moisture forming on her forehead she asked, "Do you have the heat on?" Quickly, she picked up a magazine and began fanning herself.

Madge examined the gold letters on one of Stephanie's new shirts. "No, Sweetie. We wouldn't need to keep the place warm in May," she affirmed, matter-of-factly.

Examining her freshly done nails, Stephanie suddenly became excited. "Guess what? I ate dinner with Brit and Nan this evening, right. And oh-my-god, I ate this salad with pecans and like, green plum dressing. It was really tart and tasted totally weird," she paused. "But in a good way. Anyway, we shopped for these irresistible jeans then talked with some really cute guys at the mall.

"This one guy had this fabulous, like, curly red hair." She held her palms upward and rubbed her fingertips together as if sifting his hair through her fingers. "He was totally, oh-my-god, I do mean totally, delicious!" The excitement in Stephanie's voice dropped an octave. "And what was I wearing? This..." Disgusted, she raised the hem of her short skirt and shook it. "...outdated crap! I will be *so* glad when I turn seventeen," she declared. "Then dad will let me go on vacation with Brit's family to Paris. When I get back, I will be wearing *the* latest styles."

As Stephanie prattled on, Madge finally stood up. Her arms were loaded with crinkling bags that almost covered her dark brown eyes. "You're growing up too fast, young lady. Yesterday," she said affectionately. "You were in diapers." Her weary eyes narrowed into a warm smile.

Annoyed, Stephanie glared at Madge. "Please, Madge. Let's *not* discuss it, okay?" Reaching for the remote control, Stephanie carelessly pushed her purse aside, spilling the contents on the carpet. "Garh!" she nipped. "I hate it when this happens!" Stephanie reached downward for her purse. She hesitated and frowned. "You know, I'm feeling kinda dizzy." After regaining her balance she raked the contents back into the purse.

From the corner of the room Madge stated earnestly," I hope you aren't trying to get sick, Honey."

"Yeah, me too." Stephanie felt her forehead. "If you're still cleaning my closet, I'll just get a bite to eat and, like, watch television down here." Grasping the remote, Stephanie started to surf the channels. "I'm too worn out to climb the stairs right now."

Stephanie heard Madge's voice from behind the mountain of shopping bags. "Okay, Sweetie." Balancing the bags, Madge trudged diligently up the stairs to put away Stephanie's new things.

The television was blaring loudly when Madge completed her task and prepared for bed. Because the television was so noisy she couldn't rest. Madge assumed Stephanie was still awake. "That child knows she should be in bed." Preparing to go downstairs Madge tied the sash of her robe. She walked to the edge of the stairs and looked down on the living area. Unsure if Stephanie was still awake, Madge used her cane for balance as she cautiously made her way down each step.

The hollow chime of the grandfather clock stopped to reveal it was now two o'clock. Madge made her way toward the sofa. "My goodness, that girl has fallen asleep." She crept slowly toward Stephanie. Sitting down on the sofa, Madge shook her. "Wake up, Sugar. You need to get in bed."

Stephanie pouted. "Let me sleep here tonight Madge, okay?" She turned her flushed face from Madge's view. "I don't feel very well." Stephanie shifted her body on the sofa and turned onto her side. "I shouldn't have eaten that green plum dressing on my salad." She grimaced. "I can still taste it. I knew it tasted awfully weird." She rubbed her stomach. It was hot to the touch. "I don't feel well at all."

Madge felt of Stephanie's forehead. "Honey, you have a fever. What time did you eat that crazy salad?"

Stephanie's Emerald Fever

Stephanie moaned. "I think it was around six or so."

"I need to call your parents." Madge slowly rose from the sofa and reached for the phone.

Suddenly, Stephanie boomed, "Don't call them, Madge!" She whined softly. "They're on vacation and they already think I get sick on purpose when they leave."

"Well," Madge pondered. "I'm getting the thermometer and, if your fever is high, I'm calling your parents and there will be no argument! They left the number to their hotel in the kitchen."

Getting up from the sofa, Stephanie walked uneasily upstairs. "They wouldn't care anyway," she muttered, holding her lurching stomach.

From the kitchen Madge called, "You do seem to catch whatever's in the wind when they're away, Sugar."

Stephanie yawned. "Yeah right." She wobbled up the stairs fighting back repulsive waves of nausea.

Stephanie was sitting on the side of her bed when Madge arrived. After turning down the ear piercing rock music, she placed the thermometer in Stephanie's mouth. Immediately, it started to beep. Madge removed the thermometer. "102!" She put the thermometer away. "I'm getting you something for that fever and I'm calling your parents. A high fever could fry your brain, young lady! And I'm not taking any chances."

Stephanie reached for the top to her pajamas. Slipping it over her head, she licked her dry lips. "'Fry your brain.' I guess that's just some of your weird plantation humor."

"Plantation humor?" Madge was baffled. "What on earth has gotten into you, girl? You've always been a spiteful little thing, but recently you seem to be lashing out at me for no good reason. Now, I demand an apology."

"Me, apologize?" Stephanie stood by the side of the bed. She opened the top drawer of her nightstand pulling out a hairbrush and clip. "What I meant was, don't you, like, have some cotton to pick?" Carefully, she tossed her aching head forward and briskly brushed her hair.

While Madge held her heart, a gasp stole her next breath, "What tha..."

Gathering her hair into her hands, Stephanie twisted and pinned it with a clip. "That is what you were born to do, isn't it?" She raised a brow to underline her statement.

Madge faced Stephanie sternly. "Why Stephanie Denise Andrews, how dare you! We just had this discussion before your parents left."

Stephanie's Emerald Fever

Sitting on the bed beside Madge, Stephanie violently kicked off her fluffy slippers. They landed across the room near the bookshelf.

Blinking, Stephanie scrunched up her pointed nose and waited for Madge's reply to her biting comment.

With narrowed eyes and tightly drawn lips Madge admitted, "Yes, it is true. My great-grandmother was a slave and yes, she did pick cotton on the Andrews' plantation. However, your family felt I was good enough to raise your father, and he felt I was good enough to raise you.

"Furthermore, neither your father nor your grandfather has ever owned a single slave! I am connected to your family by time and circumstances — not slavery!"

Stephanie yawned drowsily, picked up her stuffed unicorn and tossed it lazily into a nearby chair. "You say that garbage all the time."

Madge placed her brown face directly in front of Stephanie's. "Unlike you, your father has never disrespected me in any way!"

"Really. Oh-my-god!" Stephanie chuckled. "We're talking about disrespect again?" Stephanie elevated her voice mockingly. "You're not going to get on your soap box again are you?"

She crossed her recently tanned arms. "Don't you think you're getting carried away with this respect thing. After all, your family tree does have roots in slavery." Stephanie whispered quietly. "It's all getting a little stale, Madge. Don't you think?"

With a look of utter horror, Madge rose from the bed. She pulled her robe tightly around her shoulders. "I told you about my ancestors so you could understand me better. I will not stand here and listen to this nonsense." Madge started to walk away but stopped. "I respect your parent's methods of discipline, but I feel they're much too lenient with you."

When Madge reached the door, she turned. "You were born with white skin and I was born with black skin. I'm not ashamed of that fact. You would not be so quick to judge if you were born with black skin like mine."

Boorishly rolling her eyes toward the ceiling, Stephanie spoke. "Skin like yours? Like that'll happen!" She pulled back her pink comforter and crawled into bed. After pulling the covers across her lap, Stephanie fluffed her pillows then leaned against them.

Staring at Madge intensely, she teased, "All we ever hear from you people is that something is unfair."

Madge held her temper. Calmly, she stated, "Sweetheart, who told you those things? You didn't learn that kind of behavior from your father."

Placing both palms on the bed, Stephanie leaned forward and yelled, "Hello! In case you hadn't noticed, my name is Stephanie, not Stephen!"

Stephanie continued her tirade. "Let's run down the list, shall we? Just last week, Nan's father's store was robbed. Guess who did it? A black man! Christopher had his car stolen this week. Guess who did it?" She held up two fingers. "*Two* Black men! And let's not mention the fact that *all* the black girls at The Burger Boy are loud, obnoxious and rude!

"And today—just this afternoon! Some black store manager threatened to kick us out of the store. We were just having a little fun trying on stuff. A couple of things got torn. We were laughing about it." She shrugged. "I would have paid the woman but she gotta tude and stuff. Then she said *we* were too loud and destructive, so she asked *us* to leave! I didn't say anything to that frog-face woman. She said if we didn't leave the store, she would, like, call the cops! I didn't believe her and told her so. Guess what? She *called* the cops! It isn't even her store," she admitted. "I'm just getting fed up with this whole black thing!"

Madge interrupted. "Stephanie Denise Andrews, you were asking for it—tearing up that woman's garments! As for the girls at The Burger Boy, there is no excuse for acting inappropriately in public! Now, based on the things you've told me, you can't say that all black people are bad. Plus, you know better than to act like that in public!"

Stephanie hacked. "Well, I've got more examples than you have time, sister. Plus, I just think things were simpler when there were slaves — slaves were *made* to be respectful!"

Madge's eyes widened and she bit her lip. "What in the…"

Suddenly, Stephanie's head began to pound; she placed her hands on her temples and lightly massaged them. Quieting her voice, she demanded, "Get me something for this wicked headache, will you?"

Madge's expression became grave. "Well, that explains your nasty attitude," she chastised. "You've been acting a fool in public again! We *will* discuss this later." She walked out of the door, quietly closing it behind her.

When Madge returned, her expression was devoid of emotion. She gave Stephanie the capsule for her headache and a glass of water. Stephanie held the pill in her hand. "Must you stand over me?" she chided. "I'm not an infant you know." She tossed the pill into her mouth, took a sip of water then turned over in bed. Pulling the comforter around her shoulders, she snuggled under her sheets. "Disappear Madge," she grumbled. Peering from beneath the comforter, Stephanie could sense that Madge was still standing by her bed. "I mean it!" she warned.

Hastily, Madge left her side and stood silently in the doorway. Stephanie started to relax and let out a hopeless sigh. Madge had let Stephanie's attitude get to her; she shook her head repentantly.

Closing her eyes as if in prayer, she whispered, "Lord, she doesn't mean the things she's saying. I'm not making excuses for anyone who makes bad decisions, but she just doesn't understand what slavery was all about. If she could walk in the footsteps of my people then she'd understand." Pulling her robe around her shoulders, she picked up her cane and hobbled downstairs to make tea. It would be a long night.

Chapter Three

An Elaborate Set-Up

*"I should have known, Madge!
So, you're behind this elaborate set-up.
Just wait until I tell my father."*

Chapter Three

Once Madge was in the kitchen, she realized what a mess Stephanie had made. After clearing the dishes, she sat down. Absently, she sipped a cup of hot tea. Stephanie's words had pierced her aging heart and her thoughts were wrapped in the swelling of their powerful sting.

While Madge nodded over her cup of cold tea, Stephanie thrashed restlessly in bed. Sweat beaded on her brow, her stomach churned, her lips were cracked and dry. Unexpectedly, Stephanie felt as if her entire body was slowly spinning. She opened her eyes and stared blankly at the ceiling. Glimpsing a framed photograph of her parents and Madge, she noticed that Madge seemed younger. Her hair was black instead of silver. As if someone had stepped on an accelerator, the queer feeling grew more intense.

Suddenly, she noticed the photograph was actually changing before her very eyes. Not only was Madge getting younger, so were her parents! Unable to withstand the spinning sensation, Stephanie closed her eyes tightly, giving in to the feeling that overcame her body. Like an unwilling guest on a treacherous carnival ride, Stephanie felt herself being hurled out of control. Tightly clenching her blanket, she slipped into a mass of distorted voices, smeared colors and vivid smells.

The lapsing of unmeasured time left Stephanie unusually tranquil so she blissfully stirred in her comfortable bed. Without warning, she felt someone shaking her, rudely breaking the peacefulness of her rest. "Wake up, Steffy!" called a small voice. The voice called once more. "Gul, you betta wake up! We gots work to do."

Stephanie, with eyes closed, muttered, "Stop shaking me. My head still hurts. Now, go away and let me rest."

The little girl continued to shake Stephanie. "You betta stop talkin' outta yore haid. Ifn you don't git up now, you gonna git it."

Stephanie frowned, her eyelids flinching. "You don't sound like yourself. You must be getting a cold." She sighed. "Go away, I tell you."

The little girl snatched the covers from Stephanie's grasp. "You asked fer it!" She giggled with covers in hand.

A very startled Stephanie sat up in bed immediately. No one had ever dared to be that cruel. Stephanie's bleary eyes beheld the gaunt form of a little black girl. Rubbing her eyes, she attempted to bring the girl into focus. When her vision cleared, she could see that the little girl's frame was horribly frail and bony legs supported her entire structure. Her black hair was a kinky disarray of knots and tangles.

"Just lovely, we have visitors," she complained. "Give my blanket back," she ordered, jerking the covers from the little girl. She blinked her eyes to erase her image. Stephanie stretched and yawned loudly. "Guest aren't allowed upstairs. You need to explain why you're in my bedroom," she demanded.

"Gul, you must be crazy wit da heat. Dis here ain't no upstairs and it shore ain't no bedroom."

"It isn't?" Stephanie looked upward. She was alarmed to see that someone had replaced her lovely textured ceiling with unfinished boards that showed signs of decay. Further investigation of the ceiling revealed a few dried onions hanging from the rafters. Nailed haphazardly to the walls were various grains of worn jagged planks. Stephanie frowned. "What tha!" She inhaled the pungent odor of burning wood. Quickly, she turned on her side and saw an old stone fireplace positioned in the rear of the room. Beside the fireplace there was a square window, having neither glass nor screen.

Turning toward the door, Stephanie noticed that a skinny, reddish-brown chicken had strolled into the dwelling. Even though it appeared diseased, it stretched its scrawny neck, spread its wings and fluffed its sparse feathers. Stephanie gasped. "Is that a *chicken*?"

Realizing that something was horribly wrong, Stephanie gawked at the little girl. Her eyes were as round as nickels and as dark as midnight. Suddenly, she fearfully scooted herself down in bed. Pulling the covers securely around her neck, she noted that they were rough and itchy. Looking down, Stephanie discovered that an old burlap quilt had replaced her soft comforter. She let out a hideous screech. "Oh, my-god! I've been kidnapped!" She pulled the burlap quilt close to her body then gathered the courage to look beneath it.

Another ear piercing squeal tore from her lips when she discovered she was dressed just like the little black girl. Her comfortable pajamas had been replaced by a tattered cotton shift. "Eeewww! Where are my clothes? What did you do with them?" she accused. Stephanie got to her knees. "Look. Whatever the amount of money, my father will pay it. Just don't hurt me."

The little girl stared curiously at Stephanie. "Ah tol' you dat eatin' dem green plums wuz gonna give you da fever. You been talkin' outta yore haid fer hours."

Stephanie gazed around the room once more; fear leaped inside her. "Oh, please—please don't hurt me! I'll give you anything you ask for."

The little girl shook her head. "You sickern' ah thought. Umma git M'dere."

Stephanie agreed. "Yes, little girl. You do just that," she urged hurriedly, "Go—go get your mother and we'll solve this little disagreement right away."

Stephanie's Emerald Fever

The little girl walked to the front porch and called to her mother who was working outside in the field, "M'dere! Come here rat now! Steffy done woked up. She done lost her mind wit da *feverrrrr!*"

Stephanie's eyes widened with horror as she watched a shadowy figure coming through the door. The woman wore a long gathered skirt that touched the floor. Her print blouse was made of light-blue cotton and on her head she wore a dark blue kerchief.

Stephanie's lips started trembling. "I should have known—Madge! So, you're behind this elaborate set-up. Just wait until I tell my father. He will be so angry with you. I demand you take me back home this instant." Folding her arms, she turned her face angrily from the woman.

The woman knelt beside the straw-filled bed tic. She placed her plump, dark brown face right in front of Stephanie's. With an impatient scowl, she suppressed her intolerance. "First of all, yungn', don't call me by my first name, it ain't respectful. And second, I ain't gonna tolerate this kinda sass from you, sick or not. I got a notion to blaze you one."

Stephanie seemed confused. "Blaze?" she discharged. "As in strike? Oh, no. That's *not* going to happen. Not in your lifetime, sweetie. I'm not your daughter and you will *not* hit me!"

The woman was puzzled but decided to humor Stephanie. "Well then, whose daughter be you?"

Becoming furious with the silly game, Stephanie blasted. "You know darn well that my mother's name is Arlene and my father's name is Stephen!"

Aggravated, the woman exploded. "You hush-up that kinda talk! We done been in enough trouble round here wit'dout you makin' up tales. Now, ifn you feel betta, you git on out there and help Unka June Bug finish pickin' them plums."

Stephanie pulled the burlap quilt around her neck. "I'm not going anyplace."

The little girl and the woman looked at each other in amazement. The woman reached for the quilt. "You looka here. Ifn you continue to sass me, I'm gonna hafta learn you some manners."

Stephanie was terrified. "Don't, Madge! What's wrong with you? And why are you guys dressed like that?"

Frustrated, the woman sneered. "Now, see here! I ain't got time for no foolishness. Umma go out here and finish hoein' these rows, and when I gits back, you and Sam betta have this here house clean."

Stephanie's Emerald Fever

"What?" cried Stephanie. "Does everyone around here have brain damage? Where is my cell phone? I'm calling my dad and getting out of here." Stephanie leaped from the bed tic. Sam looked toward the open doorway. She watched her barefoot mother as she angrily shooed the chicken out of the house and stepped gruffly off the low porch. Gathering her long skirt into her hands, she mumbled to herself. From across the yard Sam heard, "…act like you fulla mo dan them green plums."

Stephanie ran to the back window and looked out. The scent of upturned soil assailed her nose. She saw dozens of black people working in a field, plowing miles of land for planting. A soft melody embraced her as it floated on the spring breeze.

Two white men sat on horses, watching the workers. With rifles across their laps, they had to be guards of sorts. Stephanie ran to the door. She saw more houses like the one in which she awoke. They were *all* simple, run-down shacks.

Out on the yard, her bewildered eyes saw small black children who were also working. Attentively, they walked the yard, picked up small sticks then placed them into a large basket. Feathers of various breeds littered the yard as several scrawny chickens scratched the dirt in search of food.

Hearing a flapping sound Stephanie turned to see a clothes line with damp clothes waving gently in the soft breeze. Nearby, a mangy old hound dog lay sleeping under a blossoming peach tree. Startled, she wiped her eyes and turned toward Sam. "Are those, like, rabbit skins hanging across that fence?" Stephanie could hardly believe her eyes.

"Oh my, God! I've got to get out of here! Where is the car?" she asked hurriedly, "I know how to drive well enough to get out of here." With hands extended, Stephanie ran blindly through the door. She stumbled off the unsteady porch, "I've got to get out of here!"

Sam ran after her, her bare feet padding softly against the ground. "Ah know what you is gonna drive. You is gonna drive M'dere crazy. You makin' me sick jest watchin' you."

Stephanie turned sharply, "Listen, little girl. Where is this place?"

The little girl shook her head sadly. "Unka June Bug wuz right. You got da fever." She cast her round eyes toward the heavens and proceeded to explain. "Lookie," she pointed to herself. "My name is Sam and we is on Massa Andrews' plantation."

Swallowing hard, Stephanie clasped her hand over her mouth. "Andrews," she muttered. Stephanie repeated in disbelief. "Plantation. Andrews' plantation!" She was so preoccupied with her predicament she hardly noticed she was also barefooted. "If we're at the Andrews' plantation, that means we're at my father's birthplace, right? Then he must be inside the house," she brightened.

Stephanie's Emerald Fever

Sam sighed. "Gul, we ain't goin' no place. M'dere don't play none. She said clean up da house."

Chuckling wildly to herself, Stephanie blared. "Madge. Really. She wouldn't swat a gnat, she only sounds ferocious. My father will tame her."

Smirking, Sam admitted, "M'dere's strop on yore backside is gonna tame you."

A deadened expression came over Stephanie. "No one beats kids anymore. It's against the law." Looking around nervously, she confessed, "I've got to get to the house. My parents will clear up this entire mess."

A clean breeze swept past Stephanie. As if her head suddenly cleared, she noticed the southern mansion that stood in the distance. Looking toward the old mansion, she declared, "That's it. Sweet! I saw a picture of it in our family's album." Stephanie extended her arms as if to embrace its presence. "It looks like the movie set from *'Gone With The Wind'*. Look at that lush lawn and those awesome rose beds. I wonder what they look like up close. This is extraordinary! I can hardly believe we're actually here. Yesss!" she danced. "I must have slept through the entire trip."

Knowing the perils of going to the "Big House" unannounced, Sam's face contorted into a frightful scowl. Placing her hands on her bony hips, she shook her finger at Stephanie. "Jest go on. When day gits finished wit you, dare won't be 'nuff to giva decent funeral to."

As if in a trance, Stephanie walked into the cool green grass. Ignoring nature's bounty, the "Big House" was her only goal. "They're my relatives, silly," she said haughtily. "They wouldn't hurt me."

Again, Sam shook her head remorsefully. "Ah don't know what dem green plums did to you, but you need to look in da lookin' glass. You done forgot *jest* who you is."

Looking down at her dress, Stephanie blushed. "You're right. I can't go up there looking like this. They'll think I've, like, escaped from an asylum." Sam broke and ran for the tract house. Stephanie's eyes followed her, "Hey! Where are you going?"

In a few seconds, Sam returned with a broken shard from a mirror. She handed the mirror to Stephanie. Before looking in the mirror, Stephanie started to groom what she remembered to be golden strands of silken hair. Holding the mirror to her face, she blinked dark brown, cat-like eyes. With mouth agape, she gasped.

In the mirror she saw a sixteen-year-old young "black" woman. Not believing her eyes, she turned the mirror over and investigated the back. Flipping the mirror back over, she gawked at herself again. She touched her brown skin and pinched her cheek. Her dark brown eyes widened with horror as she touched the coarsely matted hair on her head. Instantly, she passed out.

Sam ran down to the barn to get Unka June Bug. He was kneeling on the ground, mending a wagon wheel when Sam approached. Running his fingers along his suspenders, he listened to Sam for a moment. Unexpectedly, he leaped to his feet, scaring the wits out of Sam.

Unka June Bug's black leather boots padded quickly across the path toward the house. Sam had to walk twice as fast to keep up with him. Almost out of breath, she explained Stephanie's strange behavior in great detail.

When they reached the house they stood over Stephanie. Unka June Bug repeated Sam's observations. "You say she say she is white?" Stroking his mustache, he twisted his mouth musingly. Constricting his round eyes, he remarked. "Dis here the worse case of the fever I ever seen." He knelt before her and picked up her arm. "Most people see demons and such. I never hear tell of nobody waking up white." He picked Stephanie up in his strong black arms. Once Stephanie was safely inside, he instructed, "Let 'er rest. Go fetch yore mama from da field."

By the time Stephanie started to wake up, darkness had arrived at the Andrews' plantation. Tired workers found refuge in their meager homes. Fumes from a burning kerosene lamp drifted heavily on the air, adding an oily flavor to the dimness of the room. Nameless silhouettes seemed to dance against the rustic, unfinished wall. The woman who Sam called 'M'dere' knelt on the floor near Stephanie. Stephanie stirred restlessly on the old bed tic. "Wake up, Steffy," she called.

In response to the softness of M'dere's voice, Stephanie opened her eyes. The dimness of the room made it difficult for Stephanie to distinguish whether or not she was in her own bedroom. Closing her eyes gently, Stephanie admitted, "Oh Madge. I had this totally disturbing dream. I dreamed that — that —" Stephanie opened her eyes. She could now see the kerosene lamp sitting on a rickety old table. She saw Sam playing quietly near the stone fireplace, entertaining herself with a homemade doll. "Oh — it's not a dream!" She hid her face from view.

"Hush, child," M'dere whispered. "You done had a bad day. Tomorrow will be betta."

M'dere got up to get a wet rag and Stephanie started to whimper. "I can't do this," she cried. "I don't understand any of this. Why is this happening to me?"

M'dere called to her. "Don't cry, baby." She rushed back to her side. Sitting beside her, she stroked her head and hummed softly. Although Stephanie was in a state of confusion, she did find comfort in her M'dere's touch.

M'dere stopped humming and whispered to her. "When you wuz born, you wuz my chocolate doll. Yore eyes is brown now. But then, they wuz black as coal. When I looked into

Stephanie's Emerald Fever

dem eyes, I wanted a good life for you. None of us belong here, honey. But, we didn't have no choice. Now, we might as well make da best of it. A brighter day is coming."

Stephanie inhaled M'dere's familiar fragrance. She looked up into the secure warmth of her gentle eyes. "How old are you?" she asked.

M'dere seemed puzzled. "Now let's see," she whispered. "I am as old as the magnolia that graces Massa Andrews' courtyard. So, I guess that makes me thirty and five years old."

Focusing on M'dere's full lips, Stephanie asked, "You mean you aren't eighty-five?"

M'dere turned Stephanie where she could see into her eyes. "Now, child. Do I look eighty-five? My haid ain't gray." She pulled a tuft of black hair from beneath her kerchief. "I still gots all my teeth." She hugged Stephanie tightly and rocked her from side to side.

Looking over M'dere's shoulder, Stephanie spied Sam playing with the doll. She seemed content. "How can she be so happy when she has nothing?"

"Happiness is in da heart, child. Tomorrow is Sunday, now go to sleep and rest."

Stephanie held on to M'dere's clothing, "You remind me of someone special."

M'dere smiled broadly. "I is somebody special. I is yore mama."

"I'm so scared." Stephanie squeezed her eyes closed and a tear ran down her brown cheek.

The next morning, Stephanie was awakened by the aroma of freshly baked biscuits. From the floor she could see that M'dere was proudly placing old chipped plates on the table. She placed the biscuits and something that looked like butter in the center of the table. M'dere also placed a tin container that held syrup right next to the butter. Stephanie had not noticed Sam lying asleep beside her. They had shared the same straw-filled bed tic. Picking up the repulsive covers with two fingers, she covered Sam as she stirred comfortably beneath them.

From the cooking area around the stone fireplace, M'dere called, "Wake up. Wash yore face and git yore sista up too. It's time for breakfast."

A brilliant idea popped into Stephanie's head but she realized she would need Sam to help her. "Wake up, Sam," she called, shaking her just a bit.

Sam lashed out. "Stop! Ah hear ya." She frowned and turned over. "What cha want?" she asked drowsily. With excitement, Stephanie explained. "Do you, like, remember when I got the fever?"

Stephanie's Emerald Fever

"Un huh," Sam whined.

"Well, I need your help. I totally can't seem to remember anything. Will you help me remember?"

"Shore ah will," she said, groggily rising from the bed tic. "M'dere say somptin' wuz wrong wit you. She said you would be betta today…but you ain't."

"I think I've lost my memory — with the fever, I mean." She smiled weakly.

Sam stretched. "And you talk funny, too. Half da time, ah don't know what you is talkin' 'bout."

Stephanie giggled. "My dad says that, too. How old are you?"

Sam glowed proudly. "Dis here is a funny game. You is sixteen and ah is eleven."

"You've got that part right. Now, where is my father?"

Shrugging her small shoulders, Sam revealed. "Our papa wuz sold 'bouta year ago. You almost never did git over dat. M'dere said dat yore spirit wuz tied to Papa's right shoe, 'cause when he left, he took yore spirit wit 'im."

Scratching her dry skin, Stephanie got up from the bed tic. "That is totally awful," she murmured.

Sam was surprised. "Dis is gonna take some gittin' use to. Hurry now, we gotta eat, den git our hair combed fer church."

Stephanie's Emerald Fever

Chapter Four

What is This Place?

"Although, I can only read English," she admitted quietly.

Chapter Four

Stephanie felt her coarse, woolen hair. She could not imagine a comb being pulled through the maze of tangles on her head. "Will it hurt?"

Sam snickered. "You is tender haided, but M'dere uses lots of hair grease."

Stephanie cringed. "Grease? In my hair? Eeeww! But why?"

"Is you stupid? It's so M'dere can comb yore nappy haid. 'Member, she washed yore haid 'fore you gots sick." Sam popped her lips. "Jest do like I do. Com'on, dis here is gonna be fun."

During breakfast, Stephanie was intimidated by the unusually large biscuits but she did whatever Sam did; tearing her biscuit, dipping it into the butter then dragging it through the ribbon cane syrup. Much to her surprise, even though there was no meat, her stomach was still satisfied.

Next, Stephanie watched as Sam sat between M'dere's knees on an upturned bucket near the fireplace. M'dere dipped her fingers into the grease then spread it on Sam's dry scalp and hair. With a comb she parted the hair into small sections and started a trail of cornrow braids. Moving from front to back, M'dere weaved her nimble fingers back and forth with a steady pace. Stephanie sat and watched the process. She was amazed that each row was identical to the first.

Scurrying up to Sam, she whispered, "Where does this grease stuff come from?"

M'dere pretended not to hear, but she could not help but let out a low chuckle. "Now Steffy, you know da answer to that. When Massa Andrews kills a fat hog, he is kind enough to throw us da scraps. Like—da ears, da foots, da brain, da inners, and da tail. We uses all dem scraps…mostly fer eatin'. We cooks da fat and melts it fer cooking. You done seen me strain grease 'til it's pure. And it don't smell like no pig neither. I puts in a drop or two of rose oil to make it smell good."

Stephanie let out a loud, "Eeeww. That is so gross!"

"Well, I don't hear you complainin' none when you rubs this grease on dem ashy legs of yoren. Makes 'em feel real good, huh? I declare, sometimes you worry me, child." M'dere reached into a large wooden bowl. She selected some fabric and tore it into thin strips. Afterwards, she tied the shredded scraps to the ends of Sam's hair.

Stephanie lifted the odd-looking hair ornaments. "What's that for?"

"It's so ah can look purdy lack dem high society ladies," Sam kidded.

Stephanie shrugged her shoulders. "But, they're only rags!"

M'dere finished tying the last rag to Sam's hair. "I suppose you gots some fine satin ribbons tucked away somewheres. Why don't you jest let me borrow one? Yore turn now." She patted the bucket. "Sit down."

Scared and moving slowly, Stephanie sat down on the bucket. What happened next was an experience she'd never forget. Stephanie would flinch and let out a cry each time M'dere put the comb near her head. M'dere locked her knees tightly around her so she could not move. With eyes tightly closed, Stephanie gnashed her teeth, cringed and wailed helplessly each time the comb was pulled through her dry hair. Under the raking force of the comb Stephanie's dry hair made an awful popping noise.

From time to time M'dere would pull torn balls of Stephanie's hair from the comb and toss it carelessly into the fireplace. "Use more of the grease!" Stephanie argued. "It won't hurt so much if you use more of the grease!"

M'dere grew weary. "Will you stop yore frettin'? You is too big fer this kinda carryin'on. Ifn you would jest be still, it won't take so long."

After what seemed like an eternity, M'dere finally finished. Stephanie had four plaited ponytails, a calico rag tied around each one. Stephanie found the piece of broken mirror that Sam had given her earlier. Looking into the glass she noticed that she had a glossy forehead. With shoulders slumped, Stephanie sighed wistfully for her own hair. Mournfully, she pushed past Sam. "It's time for church, I guess. Where are my clothes?"

Sam scurried over to a wooden box. Proudly, she lifted the heavy lid and pulled out a simple A-line dress made from flour sacks. "Dis here is yore new dress," she beamed.

Stephanie was both disgusted and disappointed. Holding the dress with two fingers, as if it were contaminated, she screeched. "Oh-my-god! It's hideous! I don't have anything else to wear?" She pushed Sam aside and continued to search the small box. "There's got to be a better dress in this box!"

Sam drew back from the box and folded her arms. "Well, umma sit here 'til you find anotha dress. Ifn you do, you must be lookin' in somebody else's box. You ain't got but two dresses, and you is wearing one."

"But, this dress is bad for my image," Stephanie moaned, slapping the dress across her shoulder. "Alright," she sighed reluctantly. "No one important will see me anyway. Are there any shoes in that box?"

"Yep, jest one."

"One pair?" Stephanie questioned, raising her brows.

"Nope, jest one shoe. 'member, we fount it down by da creek. One day we might find anotha one." Sam held the shoe in reverence. "It shore nuff is pretty."

"One shoe. Well, this is just great," she sighed bleakly.

Sam informed Stephanie. "Mrs. Sadie is makin' you some moccasins but she ain't finished yet."

"Moccasins? Well, I guess that's better than nothing."

When Stephanie looked back into the box, she saw a worn-out book beneath an old shawl. She picked up the book. "What's this?"

"Put dat back! Is you crazy?" Sam reached for the book and Stephanie held it just out of her reach.

"Excuse me, but it's only a book," she crooned sarcastically. Stephanie looked at the cover. It had strange markings where the title should be. When she opened the book, she discovered the same strange markings on the inside too. "What is this book written in? Egyptian Hieroglyphics?"

"Naw!" Sam huffed angrily. "Ain't no glip-pics. It's jesta ABC book."

"Excuse me, but I can, like, read!" Her eyes scanned the pages once more. "Although, I can only read English," she admitted quietly.

Sam stamped her foot with aggravation. "Ifn' you can read, read what dis say." Her tiny brown fingers pointed to the first page.

Stephanie tried her best to read the book, but it all seemed foreign to her. Pointing to the print, she decided to fake it. There was no way she would allow herself to be humiliated in front of Sam. "It says, ssseee th-thee d-dog," she stammered. "There must be something terribly wrong with this book."

Snatching the book, Sam jeered. "It don't say nutin' bout no dog. Ah tol' ya, you can't read! You ain't been taught yet. Now, put dis away 'fore M'dere finds out. She tol' you to git rid of dis here book months ago. We almost got caught da last time we wuz tryin' to learn to read."

Turning her face from Sam, Stephanie folded her arms. She refused to accept such an idiotic statement. "That is totally illogical. What could happen if we are, like, seen with a book?" She cocked her head to one side.

Sam went on to explain the gory details. "Well, ifn day catch us tryin' to read, day will most likely...cut out our tongue...sos we can never read anotha word to nobody."

Stephanie made a shocking discovery. Clenching her throat she said, "You mean I really can't read?"

Sam placed her hand on her hips. "You can't read nor write. You ain't suppose to," she sassed.

"This is, like, terribly ridiculous!" Uncertain of her findings, she questioned. "Are you sure I can't write or even spell?"

"Naw!" Sam shouted, hiding the book.

"I'll die, I'll simply die. No one can live without reading. It's dangerous." Humiliation drew her lips tightly as she became lost in thought. Mumbling to herself, she tried to cram her toes into the dainty shoe. Finally exploding, Stephanie stormed, "Who made *that* stupid law?"

After everyone was dressed, M'dere closed the heavy door of the tract house. Hand in hand, the three walked along, singing hymns. Much to Stephanie's surprise, she actually knew the words. As they walked along, others joined them. These people also sang the very same song. M'dere was the proudest of all. She held her head high as her bare feet kept time on the dusty road.

When the crowd reached a clearing, Stephanie saw backless wooden benches in a semi-circle. In the May heat, Uncle June Bug wore a tweed suit. Although they were outside, he greeted everyone to the house of the Lord. Holding a white handkerchief in one hand and a tattered old bible in the other, Uncle June Bug stood on an old stump and preached the Gospel.

Stephanie's Emerald Fever

Under a grove of cotton wood trees, a white man sat on a horse, chewing tobacco. Peering from under his hat, he would mop sweat and spit from time to time. Across his lap, a rifle displayed his authority. Eyeing the crowd, he listened intensely to every word spoken.

Stephanie looked at the man much too long so Sam decided to snatch her attention forward. The man spit tobacco on the ground and leered at Stephanie through narrowed eyes. Sam kicked Stephanie under the bench and leaned toward her. "Gul, you gonna git us all a good whippin' ifn you don't stop starin'. You done forgit Joshua is da overseer? He ah real bad man."

"Get real, Sam," she whispered. "Why would I, like, get a whipping just for looking?"

"Alright, den jest keep on lookin'. Day be talkin' 'bout how natural you look in ah pine box."

"Eeeww. I am *so* not looking." She shielded her face with her hand.

After a few songs, a prayer and a few words from the Preacher, June Bug, church was over. No matter how hard Stephanie tried, she just could not stop staring at Joshua.

Thoughts of her plush world flooded her mind. She wondered if Joshua could help her get home. Again, Sam noticed

Stephanie looking at Joshua. She pulled her arm to get her attention.

Sam grew angry. "Gul, ah ain't gonna warn you no mo. Ifn' dat white man comes after you, ah can't hep you. Do you understand dat?"

On the way home, cheerful songs melted into the hearts of imprisoned souls, and there was silence. Joshua sat high on his horse thoughtfully guiding it through the small crowd. Stephanie had captured his interest so he trotted near her. She let out a shriek, as he spit large wads of tobacco as close to her bare feet as possible.

Through closed teeth, Stephanie muttered. "What is he doing, Sam?"

"Ah tol' you not to look at 'im. But, yore haid is hard."

When M'dere and her family reached their home, Joshua also stopped. Spitting more tobacco on the ground, he pushed his hat backwards, exposing his weather-beaten forehead. Gruffly, he addressed M'dere. "What you got cooked in there, woman?" He waited for her reply.

As if shot in the back, M'dere stood still. "I ain't got nutin', Sah. Jesta few biscuits fer my cheerins." She turned around to face the man.

"You mean you ain't got no fried chicken?" he roared.

"No Sah. I ain't," M'dere replied timidly.

"Ifn I come inside and finds out you is hiding an apple pie or better, you know you gonna pay for that lie, gal."

"Yas, Sah. I know," she acknowledged, shading her eyes from the midday sun.

Joshua dismounted his horse and tied it to a post on the front porch.

Stephanie was furious. "Where does he think he's going?"

M'dere waved her hand behind her to quiet Stephanie. "Hush-up, yungn'. I don't need no mo of yore help."

Sam mocked, "Ah tol' you."

Just as the three entered the shaded doorway, the man stepped onto the front porch. Pushing them inside, he spit once more, this time, directly on the floor. "Let me see them biscuits you was talkin' 'bout," he ordered. After sitting his slender frame on a chair, he propped his feet upon the table, then leaned against the wall.

M'dere ushered the girls into her sleeping area behind a hanging quilt. Her eyes told them to stay put. Turning slowly, she went to get the leftover bread.

"What is he going to do?" Stephanie asked quietly from M'dere's bed tic.

"Hush up!" scolded Sam, clasping her hand over Stephanie's mouth. "M'dere said...you done-done 'nuff already."

When M'dere placed the bread, butter, and syrup in front of Joshua, he looked at the plate then looked at M'dere. His eyes narrowed with disgust. In one swipe, he violently shoved the entire meal onto the floor. "This cold stuff ain't fit for hog slop! You tryin' to poison me, gal?"

Leaping to her feet, Stephanie whispered. "Why, that cowboy wannabe! Who does he think he is?" Her voice escalated from the corner of the room. "That's, like, our dinner!"

Sam reached for Stephanie. Holding onto her dress, she pleaded with her not to move. "You don't know what you is doing. He gonna hurt you bad!"

Joshua heard the commotion. "Let 'er go!" he bellowed. "I wanna hear what she gots to say. She talkin' mighty scrappy for a scrawny little gal."

Smoldering with resentment, Stephanie rebuked the man, her bitterness drawing her closer to him. "How could you come into the home of these poor people and, like, throw their food on the floor?" Her eyes were fixed with rage.

Joshua looked at Stephanie. He appeared pensive. As if in deep thought, he stroked the scraggly hairs on his chin and rocked back and forth on the chair. Suddenly, he erupted into laughter. Joshua coughed and sputtered then slapped his knee, gasping for breath. As quickly as he started laughing, he stopped. "You got spunk. I don't know what you is sayin' but you got spunk. Did anybody tell you that spunk will get you kilt?" He spit a large wad of tobacco juice on the floor. "Git it up!"

Stephanie looked behind her then she pointed to herself. "Are you talking to me?" She looked at M'dere. Chuckling playfully, she reaffirmed. "I know he isn't talking to me."

Joshua became annoyed. He stared at Stephanie and sucked his teeth. "I said, git it up!"

Stephanie folded her arms and stood steadfast. "I don't think so."

Unexpectedly, he sprung from his chair and cuffed Stephanie in the back of her head.

Under his brute force, Stephanie went flying across the room. Unharmed, her initial reaction was shock! 'How dare he put his hands on an Andrews?' she thought. Gathering her senses she arose, unaware that Joshua was nearby. He gave her another hearty shove. This time Stephanie landed by the fireplace with a loud thud. M'dere screamed while Joshua took pleasure with his new toy, Stephanie.

"I loves dealin' with disrespectable slaves…gives me somethin' to do at the end of the day."

M'dere tried to pull the man away from Stephanie, but Stephanie refused to give up. A resentment she had never known churned in her stomach. She had been dishonored beyond all reason. As a proud descendent of Andrews' blood, Stephanie was determined to make herself known. While she was losing consciousness, Stephanie heard a blood-curdling scream tear from M'dere's lips.

Stephanie's Emerald Fever

Chapter Five

I Don't Do Windows

"Bad slave. Me? Oh yes, I recall now – that's my new persona."

Chapter Five

"Steffy. Wake up, gal." M'dere tied her apron tightly around her waist. Stephanie responded with a low groan. "Wake up, ya hear?"

Stephanie opened her eyes. Staring at the shoddy ceiling overhead, she took her time answering. "Great," she moaned. "I'm still here." She pulled herself upright on the old bed tic. "What did I ever do to deserve this? What do you want now?" Stephanie wiped her eyes and glared at M'dere.

"Gal, you done forgot yoreself again! Don't make me backhand you."

Stephanie shook her head, lazily stood up then stretched. "I've tried to tell you guys that no one beats kids anymore. I really don't think you're, like, listening to me."

"Jest git on up!" M'dere yelled intolerantly. "Now, umma tel Massa Andrews dat you is feelin' poorly and you can't go to da field today. Do you understand me, gal?"

The force in M'dere 's voice caused Stephanie to draw back and grimace. "I hear you," she replied irritated. "Garh! I hear you. That'll be fine with me I'll just lie down for a little bit longer."

"You'll do what?" M'dere wretched.

"What time is it anyway?" Stephanie asked, scratching her side.

"You know what time it is, gal! It's 5:30 and we is suppose to be ready to go to da field when Unka June Bug gits da wagon 'round. We is going to da north field today, and I need you to git thangs done 'round here. You and Sam git dat washin' done, den peel and cook dem taters fer suppa. I ain't playin' wit you, gal. It betta git done!"

Shuffling her feet, Stephanie walked slowly toward the fireplace. "Did anyone tell you I don't do windows?" she kidded.

M'dere shook her head. "My-my." She turned toward Sam who was eating breakfast. "Come on, gal. Um dependin' on you to keep dis thang outta trouble."

Stephanie raised her wet face from the washbasin. "Did you, like, call me a thing?" She patted her face dry with a large rag and yawned. "Hurry along and do your," she motioned dismissively with her hand, "field duty. I'll be right here when you get back."

"Humph!" M'dere huffed as she walked toward the door.

It was late by the time Sam convinced Stephanie to start the washing. She knew all too well the wrath M'dere could inflict upon them if their work was unfinished. Long after Sam had eaten Stephanie sat down to eat breakfast.

"Com'mon!" Sam cried pulling on Stephanie's arm. "It's almost 6:30 and we ain't even started da fir yet."

Each time Stephanie would try to take a bite of her biscuit Sam would pull her arm, therefore she could not reach her mouth. "Why is you actin' lack this?"

Finally getting a decent bite, Stephanie stopped chewing and glared at Sam. "Look, little girl. I just started trying to eat this totally cold, oversized biscuit and this," she held up a chip of dry salt bacon, "little crunchy thingy *you* call bacon. Now, I'm sitting here until I finish. I don't know anything about starting a 'fir' and I have no intentions of washing anything." She continued to chew.

Sam's eyes bulged and her mouth flew open, "What cha say?"

"You heard me," Stephanie muffed, munching slothfully on the biscuit.

"Oh, please don't say dat. M'dere will skin us boff ifn we don't git dis here work done."

After another thirty minutes of begging, Sam convinced Stephanie to help her gather things to wash. They went from track house to track house. On each porch someone had left a small bundle of washing. Stephanie had no idea they had to also wash for the other families who had gone to the field.

"Why do we need to wash all of these clothes?" she asked, sulking. "I thought we only had to wash our own clothing."

Sam stopped walking and shifted the bundle in her small arms. "Well, dat's jest selfish to jest wash yore own clothes... when day is all in da field together. We hafta wash all deez clothes."

"Are you saying that just because they're working in the field, we must take responsibility for all their clothing?"

"Yep." Sam stood motionless, "You know what? Dat fever sure done did you bad. Most likely...you gonna git us kilt wit dis kinda puttin' on."

Looking Sam sternly in the eyes, Stephanie admitted, "Look. I don't want to get anyone quote, 'kilt' unquote," she mocked. "But I really don't want to put my hands on someone's grimy clothing. If my girls saw me now they would, like, laugh me under the entire school."

As if startled, Sam looked up. "Here comes Joshua on his hoss," she teased, pointing toward the big house. "He gonna knock you out like he did last night." With her free hand, Sam pretended to hit herself on the head with her knuckles. She cocked her head to one side and jutted her tongue out the side of her mouth.

"He hit me?"

"Shore 'nuff he did. Jest like dis—whappo! Ah tried to tel' ya, but yore haid is hard."

Stephanie rubbed the tender knot on the back of her head. "I'll see to it that he's fired." Looking toward the big house she rubbed her head again.

Sam dumped the clothes into a heap. "Dats what you gits when you is a bad slave."

"Bad slave. Me? Oh yes, I recall now—that's my new persona. Well, I'll just show all of you that this slave thing is not so hard. You guys use this stuff as an excuse."

Squinting to see the sun rising, Sam confessed, "Ah don't know what you is talkin' 'bout, but da sun is risin' and we ain't started washin' yet. We ain't even bilt no fir to heat dis here wada."

Stephanie towered over Sam. Looking downwards she declared, "I don't know how to build a fire. Do I look like a Boy Scout to you?"

"Ah don't know nuttin' bout no scout," Sam grumbled. "But you always starts da fir 'fore you goes to da field. Ifn you don't start da fir under da wash pot, we can't wash." Sam's eyes scanned the entire quarters. Almost everyone had gone to the field. "Unlesson," she paused. "Unlesson, ah gits Nate to make ah fir. Nate can do anythang."

Stephanie's eyes followed Sam's gaze. Across the yard, they observed a young boy carrying a basket full of brown eggs. His feet were bare and he wore only a long white shirt. Stephanie leaned down and whispered to Sam, "Where are his jeans?"

"Huh?" asked Sam. "His jeans?" Sam shook her head, "What is you talkin' 'bout now?"

Stephanie covered her mouth with her hand and whispered to Sam. "Don't look, but he isn't, like, wearing any pants, just a long dingy shirt."

Sam picked up two sticks to place under the old, black washpot. Discouraged that Stephanie was unable to help her, she tossed the sticks to the ground. "Umma be so glad when you gits well. Um tired of tellin' you what you already know. He ain't gots no pants," she informed flippantly. "Cheerins who don't work in da field don't gits no clothes. Boys gits two shirttails ah year, and dats all."

Stephanie could not imagine the guys at school wearing only shirts.

"Umma tel' you dis again." She held two fingers in Stephanie's face. "On dis here plantation guls git two dresses ah year and no shoes. When you gits ageable, like twelve or so, you works in da field...den you gits three changing clothes and one pare of shoes ah year."

"Well, where are my shoes? I'm old enough to have a pair."

Sam stared at her in disbelief. "Gul, dem shoes wuz too li'l. M'dere give 'em to Addie, da new gul. Ah done tol ja, Mrs. Sadie is gonna make—"

"Well that just sucks. What am I going to wear until then?" Stephanie picked up an old dress, beholding the amount of sewn-on patches.

Shunning Stephanie's comments, Sam added. "Wear what you is wearin' now." She placed her hand on her small hips. "Now, is you gonna listen or talk?"

"Garh! Don't be so sensitive," Stephanie frowned. "I'm like, listening."

"Ah was bout to say you gits mo food when you is ageable."

"More food?" Stephanie asked concerned. "Why is that?"

Sam shrugged her shoulders. "It ain't much food but slaves need day strength to work hard. It ain't much, ah tel' ya...jesta crocka meal and flour fer cookin'." Sam kicked the clothing into a pile. "When you is bad we don't gits no food. Like ifn M'dere wuz to run away to Sweet Freedom—Massa Andrews wouldn't give usn no food 'til she caught and brung back."

"Look, Sam," Stephanie spurned. "This entire slavery thing is, like, making me ill. I don't like being referred to as a slave. I am free, Caucasian, and very well off. I just need to make you understand that. Get real! I live in New York!"

After Stephanie finished her sentence, Sam rolled her round eyes toward the heavens. "Nate!" she called loudly. "Come 'ere. We is needin' yore hep." Sorting the clothes for washing, she grumbled to herself. "'bout to git on my nerves wit dat kinda talkin'."

As Nate approached, Sam's eyes tapered sharply. She stared venomously at Stephanie. "Ah know you is biggern me, but ifn you tel' Nate you is white, umma whop you myself." Tossing the last piece of clothing into a pile, Sam snorted angrily. "Talkin' too much is 'gainst da rules. And da elder folks will shore nuff beat you fer dat. Do you want Mama Bell or Mrs. Sadie on yore backside? Ifn you don't, you betta mind yoreself and keep them lips of yourn closed."

"Okay—okay," Stephanie relented, holding a feisty Sam at arm's length.

With the basket of eggs in his hand and shirttails flapping in the morning breeze, Nate ambled toward the girls. His brownish-black hair was a tangled mass of miniature corkscrews. Positioned oddly in his head were deep-set eyes that hid behind a jungle of tight lashes. As if he had a whistle in his cheeks, his lips carried a puckered appearance. "Kpele. She ara le?"

Sam replied, "Kpele."

Nate asked, "Ara aburo re ko i ti ya ni?"

Stephanie was confused by what her ears heard. "What tha?"

Sam giggled. Hiding her mouth with her hand she whispered, "Beni. O je osan ti ko i kpon."

Nate gazed at Stephanie. He looked at the top of her head then his eyes swept down to her feet. "O yato."

Insulted, Stephanie screamed. "Speak English!"

Sam was startled. "Ah forgits. We is not speakin' Anglish. Most likely...dat ah be da death o' me. Unka June Bug done warned me 'bout dat, but ah can't tels when ah ain't speakin' Anglish."

Frustrated, Stephanie stamped her feet and stormed, "Just light the darn fire!"

Nate smiled. "Ko gbadun."

"What did he say?" she inquired. "Did he just call me dumb?"

Tossing the dirty clothes into the pot, Sam receded. "Naw. Now, go git some mo wada fer dis here wash pot, while ah gits the rub board."

Stephanie sighed. "Where do I get this water?"

Sam bit her bottom lip. "At da well!" she snapped. She pointed toward the big house. "Da well?" she emphasized with both brows raised. Handing Stephanie an empty bucket she pushed her in the right direction.

Stephanie smiled deviously. "I'm going to the mansion? Excellent! Will they ever be glad to see me."

Chapter Six

What Happened to My Beautiful Voice?

Perhaps, slaves didn't yearn for careers,
but her future was sealed with the fashion industry.

Chapter Six

Just as Stephanie got the big house in her sight, she heard an old man calling out. "Ifn you going to the Big House, take dese here plums. They is waitin' on 'em." Stephanie turned to see an old man limping toward her. He was carrying a large bucket of fragrant ripe plums.

With smiling yellow eyes, he stated proudly, "These here gonna make some awfully good plum jelly. Mama Bell makes the best plum jelly in this whole era. Folks comes from miles around just to buy it." Limping up to Stephanie, he placed the bucket in her other hand. "Now, don't you spill none of 'em, you hear?"

Standing numbly, Stephanie looked at the bucket in her hand then she looked at the old man. He was darker than any Black person she had ever seen. With a curious glower, Stephanie started, "Who the heck are—"

Coming from behind, Sam butted in. "Jacob! Mornin' to ya. Umma go wit Steffy to take deez here plums. She been kinda ailin'."

Jacob scratched his scraggly gray beard and curled his pink upper lip at the corner. "I did hear 'bout that. They said she et a buncha them old half-green plums and got the fever. They calls it the "Emmaral Fever." They said the "Emmaral Fever" makes you see demons and such. They say you go outta your haid for a spell, but when you gits well you done learnt a valuable lesson." He stared at Stephanie. "Now, that ain't happened to you none, has it?"

Not replying, Stephanie simply stared at the man. Her eyes narrowed with overtones of disrespect. She noticed that the pockets were torn off his jacket and he had no pockets on his pants. "Haven't you ever, like, heard of The Salvation Army? They can give you better rags than that! What happened to your pockets anyway?" she asked.

Jacob turned his back toward Stephanie. Looking at Sam, he used his thumb to point over his shoulder at Stephanie. "It's the fever, ain't it?"

"Yas, Sah. It's da fever."

Jacob decided to humor Stephanie. "Now, you ain't forgot it's my job to take care of dese be-u-ti-ful grounds have you?" He hugged himself tightly. "I loves them like they wuz a fine-lookin' lady." He took off his dusty jacket and handed it to Sam.

Sam knew that Old Jacob was going to dance for a spell so she smiled. Old Jacob started to walk around Stephanie, her eyes followed his movement. "So, you wonder why I ain't gots no pockets?" he asked cheerfully. Raising his bad foot high into the air, Old Jacob stomped a beat on the moist ground then he started to prance. "You wonder why I ain't gots no pockets? Well, I ain't gots no pockets," he sassed. "Sos I can't steal from the Massa. Ask me if I would steal food and the answer would be, ya sah."

As he danced, he studied the unresponsive expression on Stephanie's face. "People steals food when they work at da 'Big House'. I don't steal 'nough to feed a church mouse." He kicked his feet high into the air. "I'm too old to work in da field, so I cleans up the yard and such. I keeps it lookin' be-u-tiful and thank you very much."

Unmoved by his buoyant demeanor, Stephanie stared motionlessly at the prancing man. Dismissing his sociable gesture, she heaved, "Whatever!" Groaning, she returned her thoughts to the lure of the 'Big House'.

Out of breath, Jacob turned toward Sam and motioned toward Stephanie with his thumb. Mocking her spiteful behavior, he placed his hand on his hip. "Whatever!" he mimicked, with a benevolent grin.

Recalling the taught manners of her people, Sam showed her appreciation to Old Jacob. She kissed the back of his hand, gave him back the jacket and smiled. Lowering her head in reverence she slowly backed away from Old Jacob's presence, pulling an ill-mannered Stephanie along with her. Together, they turned and walked quietly away. When they were out of hearing range, Sam struck Stephanie on the arm with her small fist then snatched the bucket of plums.

"Ouch! What was that for?" she asked, holding her arm.

Walking briskly, Sam snorted, "You done dispected, Old Jacob. You outta be shame of yoreself."

Stephanie shuddered. "He should be ashamed of himself. Someone needed to tell him that he needs serious government assistance. Eeww," she squealed, looking behind her. "Doesn't he own a toothbrush? There are, like, crumbs between his teeth."

"Ah toothpick," Sam added, pushing Stephanie off balance.

"A what?" she asked, regaining her balance.

"Jest never you mind. Com'on!"

The girl's conversation faded into the morning dew as Sam told Stephanie of the awful day Old Jacob lost his toes. "Mrs. Sadie tol' M'dere dat when Old Jacob wuz a young man he wuz mighty proud. He wuz da royal son of ah king and he ain't wanna be no slave. Massa Andrews trusted him to work on da north field...but when it come time to load da wagon, Old Jacob wuz gone. He had done run away to Sweet Freedom. Massa Andrews gots so mad dat he puta boun'tee on Old Jacob's haid. He said when Old Jacob was caught he wuz gonna taught him a lesson."

In disbelief Stephanie interrupted. "Oh, come on! He had to have done more than that. He must have stolen something."

"Naw, he ain't steal nuttin', jest hisself and his freedom."

"Oh," Stephanie sighed sadly.

"Now, it wuz tol' to me dat when day fount Old Jacob, he wuz livin' in da woods. He had done built him a shed and was eatin' ah might good. Oh, but day beat 'im and beat 'im till he bled lika stuck hog. Den day tooka axe and cut da toes clean offn his feet."

"Stop!" Stephanie's hand shot up instinctively. "I've heard enough." She could imagine Old Jacob's toes detached and wiggling in the dirt.

Chirping birds and mischievous squirrels entertained the two as they finished their journey to the well in total silence. Once they made it to the well, Sam pushed the covering from the top and let the bucket down into the water. "Hey!" Stephanie's voice echoed, "This is deep!"

"You gonna fall in," Sam warned, pulling hard on the thick rope. "Den day gonna hafta clean da well after day gits you out." She laughed wildly. "You needa bath anyways." She poured the fresh clean water into the bucket and immediately tossed it back for another refill.

Stephanie indiscreetly smelled under her arms. "You are right. I do smell…like onion rings." She turned around to face the broad side of the house. "We need to take these plums inside, right? I need to prep myself for this." She inhaled deeply.

"They will probably see how much I look like a family member and ask me to spend the night."

"Oool," Sam giggled. "You shore is funny. Most folks 'round here looks like family members."

Standing by the well, Stephanie could see clearly into the kitchen window. She saw two large black women stirring around in the kitchen. "Which one is Mama Bell?" she asked.

"Mama Bell is da older bright-skinned one," Sam exposed, pointing toward Bell. "Da otha one is Addie."

"Okay. Bright-skinned it is." She picked up the bucket of plums then started for the kitchen steps. "I hope Addie enjoys wearing my shoes." Under Stephanie's feet were steps that led to the back door they were painted a festive red. An intricately carved banister painted red and white was attached to the left side of the step.

Sam gingerly rubbed the well-designed banister. "Jest cause you can't 'member, M'dere tol' us dat our Papa made deez here steps. She said he wuz good at his work. Dat's why he brung so much money to Massa Andrews when he was sole."

"Will you stop talking like that? You've depressed me all the way from the house. I'm going to need therapy when I get home. Now, stop it will you?"

Stephanie's Emerald Fever

Sam knocked on the door. Stephanie held the bucket of plums tightly in her fist and grinned. Excitement danced in her heart; her eyes widened with anticipation. Anxiously waiting, she listened as the sound of quick and lively footsteps neared the door. Surely, someone would recognize her.

When the door opened, a white woman appeared. She was wearing a light blue dress with a wide hoop beneath. As she stood before them, she smiled. With a spirited southern drawl she sparkled, "Oh, you have the plums. I've been waitin' for them." She turned toward the kitchen area. "Bell, the plums have finally arrived! Come and get them, Shugah."

Jeweled tucking combs held the thick brown hair that lay in ringlets around her straight shoulders. The woman was around fifty years old. She had an animated voice that was both jovial and light. After hearing English broken into so many pieces, Stephanie welcomed her tone and grammar. How elegant her dress was ample fabric draped gracefully over a hoop. A tight corset accentuated her tiny waist. Stephanie was bursting with enthusiasm. Her eyes merged with the soft brown eyes of the woman. This had to be The Mrs. Andrews...the diva of the Big House.

Her clear brown eyes fell upon Stephanie. Somehow she reminded her of Martha Washington. Like a queen pleased with her court, the woman smiled down on her. Stephanie smiled back broadly; exposing what she thought was expensive dental work. "Bell, get these girls a teacake. They look like they could use a bite." The woman walked away from the door, leaving a trail of rose-scented perfume behind.

Stephanie placed her foot upon the next step then stepped fully inside the kitchen. Sam pulled her back with a sharp tug. "What is you doin'?" she whispered.

Ignoring Sam's insistent tug, Stephanie whispered back. "The lady said we could have some tea bread or something. Let me go," she insisted. "She knows me. I can see it in her eyes."

Anxiously, Stephanie snatched her dress from Sam's grasp. "Stop pulling on me Sam!" Mesmerized by thoughts of lavish comforts, she babbled. "Oh-my-god! Did you see that totally awesome dress?" She held her hand to her chest as if she was struck speechless. "What do you think—three-four thousand dollars, maybe?" She sighed excitedly. "Come on. We've got to get inside. There's more to see!"

"No!" Sam cried, pulling her back. "Umma get a stick and whop you on da haid. You 'bout to git us kilt!"

"No one is going to get killed. You've just got to know how to handle the old gal." She peered inside the house again. "Now, watch a pro in action."

The aroma of fried chicken and cooking vegetables invited her inside the kitchen. She could hear someone playing the piano in an adjacent room. "You hear that?" she asked eagerly. "It's Beethoven! They have a piano in the next room. I can play the piano."

Sam dropped her head, turned around, and plopped herself down on the bottom step. "Ah can't tel' ya what to do. You is too hard haided fer me. Jest go on," she said sadly. "Umma tel' M'dere ah tried."

Stephanie looked down at Sam. "Oh, stop being such a drama queen," she chastised. "I only want to see the piano." From where she was standing she could see that Bell was pulling a large jar made of crockery from the cupboard. Elation of her final destination coursed through her veins as she stroked the wainscoting and felt the wall leading to the kitchen.

From the corner of her eye, Bell witnessed the entire incident. The kitchen was hers to safeguard. She stepped in front of Stephanie. With a rich Cajun accent, Bell asked, "And whar do you tink you are going, little gerl?" Being a large woman, Bell towered above her.

"Ah, well I," Stephanie stammered looking sheepishly up into the angry folds of Bell's round face. "I heard music," she stuttered.

"You know betta dan to come into dis house. I have a good mind to tell yore Mada." Bell raised her hand to swat Stephanie. "You are too old for dis kinda ting." She swatted Stephanie hard across the back. The unexpected blaze of burning skin caused her to wince beneath the pain. "Imagine, a gerl like you. You should be getting ready for de marriage instead of playing deez bebe games!"

The word "marriage" stung Stephanie as hard as the swat from Bell's humongous hand. Could it be possible that she was a good age to marry? The thought made her quiver. Perhaps, slaves didn't yearn for careers but her future was sealed with the fashion industry.

The woman Stephanie felt had to be Mrs. Andrews returned. She noticed that Stephanie was clenching her shoulder, her face contorted in pain. "What happened here, Bell?" she quizzed, looking Stephanie over with concern.

Bell bellowed, "Dis little gerl was trying to sneak into de house. When her Mada returns from de field, I will see to it dat she is punished."

The woman's face softened with compassion. "Now, Bell. There is no need for that. What could she possibly want?" She gazed at Stephanie with the sympathy usually given to a stray pup. "Bell, I know that yore daddy was Franch, God rest his soul. But yore mama is Af-i-can. You've lived among them. Can't you understand a little bit of their language?"

Bell stood with her plump hands on her wide hips. Angrily, she dusted her hands on her apron. "Humph! She said she heard de music."

Surprised, the woman turned toward Stephanie. "Is that right, Shugah?" She reached down and touched Stephanie's beaming brown face. Cupping the grinning face in her soft hands she added, "I heard that these savages love music. It calms them down." Looking into Stephanie's eyes she asked, "You like the pretty music?"

Stephanie looked into the woman's eyes. Her skin was soft and untouched by the consequences of hard labor. Stephanie had to make her realize that she was also an Andrews. She was going to show her that she was intelligent and not like the other slaves. "Mo gbadun orin yen," she said impatiently, "orin yen!"

Clearly aggravated the woman spurned. "Speak Anglish, Dear."

Stephanie tried again. "I like the music." But what the woman heard was, "Mo gbadun orin yen." Clearing her throat, she tried again, this time more slowly, "Ah...likes da music." Stephanie scowled. *'Who said that? What has happened to my beautiful voice? It sounds so coarse and scraggly. I know I can speak English.'* Once again, she tried to speak. "Aso re lewa pupo."

The woman appeared aggravated. "Shugah, I don't know what you is trying to say. You know you're supposed to use Anglish, when addressing me. It's only right and proper."

Stephanie looked down at Sam who was now waiting in the grass. "Why can't she understand me?"

Sam snickered, but said nothing. Mrs. Andrews became frustrated and started to walk away. Shunning Stephanie, she grumbled, "These savages, I do declare!"

Soon, Bell gave Stephanie the teacakes and slammed the door behind her.

With the smell of fried chicken embedded in her dress, Stephanie turned toward Sam. Picking up the water bucket she asked, "Why couldn't she understand me? And don't tell me you don't know."

Sam was laughing so hard that she could hardly stand up. At last, she revealed. "You ain't learnt good Anglish yet. You been in da field." She held her side in laughter. "Dat wuz pity ful!" Sam staggered along the trail and repeated. 'Ah likes da music.' What you say, Steffy? 'Ah likes da music!' Say dat again, it sound so funny!"

Stephanie's body grew rigid with anger. Although she carried the heavy water bucket, embarrassment made her knees weaken. "This is not amusing at all. Why didn't you tell me I couldn't speak English very well?" She huffed. "I know why. You thought it would be cute to watch me make a fool out of myself."

Sam stopped laughing. "Ah tried to stop ya, but yore haid is so hard. M'dere say ifn you gits knocked on yore ears, you can hear betta."

"Oh, shut up! We still have clothes to wash." Stephanie mumbled to herself. *'Knocked on your ears'. What kind of gibberish is that? These people are driving me to antidepressants!'*

L.J. Maxie

Chapter Seven

You Ain't Nuttin' Special 'Round Here!

"He'll have you sold 'fore mornin' ifn you ain't careful."

Stephanie's Emerald Fever

Chapter Seven

A̲s the day went on, the girls worked over the hot wash pot. They thromped the clothes with a stick and pulled them out the hot water. Using a brick of homemade lye soap, they lathered the clothing then rubbed them on the sturdy rub board. After they had finished rinsing the clothes, they wrung them and hung them up to dry.

Although Stephanie was not speaking to Sam, she was still grateful to have her around. From time to time Old Jacob kept an eye on the two, especially Stephanie, who was 'acting a might daft.'

When M'dere came home from the field she didn't feel well. Luckily, she found the clothes washed and dinner almost cooked. She moved lethargically around the kitchen as she finished cooking the dinner. Sam could almost swear her mother seemed too weak to stand up. Without warning, M'dere simply retired early.

After admitting to Sam that she had never cooked real potatoes over a fire, Stephanie felt a little embarrassed. Sam had no idea what a microwave was and found the entire concept impossible to believe. Nevertheless, she enjoyed Stephanie's strange tales. When they finished most of their work Sam took Stephanie on a memory tour of the quarters, showing her points of interest.

Sam was concerned about M'dere. She never missed after supper activities and deeply enjoyed the brief moments when tired family members sat around the fire. But on this night, no one heard M'dere's contagious laughter.

Sam told Stephanie that this was also her favorite part of the day. Family and friends gathered to perhaps tell stories or dance. Some people worked by the firelight. They made comforts for their family, like quilts or soft moccasins for those without shoes.

Laborious rubbing on the rub board had caused abrasions on Stephanie's knuckles. She massaged her hands with a salve that Sam provided. After putting the salve on her arms Stephanie tried to ignore the minor burns she sustained while cooking.

Stephanie sat on a stump between Nate and Sam. The damp soil felt weird to her feet as she wriggled her toes in the moist warmth of a hard day's end.

Curious about how moccasins were made, Stephanie dared watch Mrs. Sadie at her craft.

Mrs. Sadie's heavy frame sat on a wooden bench. Although she worked quietly by the firelight, she heard and knew everything that was said or done. With her large needle, a special thimble and a thick cord, Mrs. Sadie had no obligations to make hand sewn moccasins. Rather, she made them as a labor of love. Stephanie observed that Mrs. Sadie's skin was a bittersweet chocolate. She was almost as large as Bell and perhaps twice as mean.

Old Jacob sat whittling away on a sugar cane pole. He cut the cane into four-inch portions and gave everyone a share. When the cane reached Stephanie, she held it, unsure of what to do next. After watching the others, she reluctantly peeled back the tough exterior of the cane and bit into the delicate sweetness the ragged core had to offer. "It's sweet," she admitted, sucking the nectar from the core. "This is too cool," she whispered to Sam.

"Hush! It's time fer Old Jacob to tel' his story."

"This moist air is going to wreak havoc on my hair," Stephanie complained, tightening the rags that held her platted hair together.

Old Jacob started with a song. He sang loudly, then he sang softly. He moaned a while then he started his story: "When da sky wuz blue like the wada of the ocean and the land wuz full wit bounty, there lived a mighty king. This wuz not just any king. He wuz the mightiest of all kings.

"One night he wuz awaken by a strange dream. He tried to remember da dream. He told da dream to his many wives, but none of them could tell him what his dream meant.

"So, the king told his dream to da elders: 'There wuz a land where da mighty lion lived,' he said. 'This wuz a good lion and his people served him well. One day he found that da witch doctor had betrayed him. He learned that he wuz trying to trade his cattle to other villages. The mighty lion knew that he should put da witch doctor away for this act of treason. But, everyone knows that you cannot put a witch doctor away because his magic is too strong. He would only rise up against the mighty lion and kill him.

"So, da clever lion saw opportunity to send da witch doctor far, far away on a big boat where he could never return to da village. All of da people wuz happy about the lion's decision to put da witch doctor away. But, something other ideas come to his haid.

"'What if I send all of the bad people away? If I put them on this boat then my kingdom would be rid of evils. Only da good people would remain in da village.'

"So, when the big boat came to da island, the clever hyena spoke to the mighty lion. 'Give us your evils and we will punish them. In return, we will give you many precious things.'

"The mighty lion liked this idea. So, each time da hyenas came to da village da mighty lion gave him da evils in exchange for precious things.

"One day the clever hyenas tried to figure out a way to trick the lion into giving them more of da evils. 'We punish da evils from sun up to sundown. We make them work hard in da field,' they say.

"But dese evils were worth more than da treasure da mighty lion received. When the mighty lion found out that he had been tricked, he stopped giving da hyenas his evils. But, da hyenas wuz not happy. They needed the evils, because da evils brought them much money.

"They asked the lion for da evils again, and the mighty lion said, 'I will keep my evils and punish them myself.'

"By then the hyenas had become so greedy for da evils that they attacked da village. They not only took da evils, they also took the kings sons and daughters. To this, da king was most unhappy. His village was destroyed and his people taken away in chains.

"The mighty lion wept that he had given da hyenas the first evils, which made them thirst for da rest. The lesson of da story: Deal with yore own evils, and don't trade them to anyone else."

The night was still when Old Jacob finished his story. Although Sam had heard it many times, she still liked to hear Old Jacob tell about the kings and queens in the land where the sky is as blue as the ocean.

One by one, people drifted away to rest their tired bodies. Stephanie wasn't sleepy so she sat by the fire and stared into the flames. The fire flickered and crackled before her, sending short bursts of smoke upward. Like the smoke, Stephanie's mind drifted back to her own world. She recalled walking into her apartment, burdened by packages. She recalled the gleam in Madge's eyes whenever she came home at the end of her school day. Now it was clear to Stephanie that Madge truly loved her.

Lifting her eyes toward the starry night sky, she saw Brit's excitement about the new jeans they had purchased. Of course, they teased her about the new guy she met at the mall. His eyes were so hypnotic that he had the ability to charm almost any girl; and Stephanie was the girl he had chosen to charm.

She thought of her parents and the fun they must be having without her. Then it occurred to her…she had been such a brat that no one probably missed her at all, especially Madge. Stephanie could almost smell the fresh clean fragrance of her sheets and she wished for the comforts of home. She had no idea how long she had been away and absolutely no idea of how to return home. A gentle tap on the shoulder startled her, "Huh?"

When Stephanie turned around, she looked up into the gorgeous green eyes of a young man, perhaps sixteen or seventeen, years old. "Oh-my-god! You scared me." Stephanie was astonished. The guy seemed oddly familiar, but she had no idea why.

"I been watchin' you all night, Miss Steffy. You ain't looked at me once."

"Well, I've been preoccupied," she admitted, nervously wiggling her knees back and forth.

"Pre-what?" The guy's eyes softened.

"Nothing," she said shyly.

The guy came closer. His caramel colored skin felt warm as he neared her. "You act like you ain't got well yet. I heard 'bout the fever. They say it take a while 'til you yore old self again."

"Thanks for that information," she acknowledged, blushing.

"Yas, sah. You is still ailin'," he declared, absently searching the sky. "I can tell by yore talkin'. But, I ain't sked of you none. You can talk to me." He sat down on the warm rock where Sam had recently been sitting. Raising his hat, he pulled at a broken twig tangled in his curly red hair. "They say these dreams feel real to ya. Tell me 'bout 'em."

Stephanie lowered her head remorsefully. "I can't tell anyone what I saw in the dream. I guess it was just a bad dream."

"Tell me what you saw," he prodded, pulling out his knife and a whittling block.

"Can I trust you?"

"'Corse you can. They don't call me Honest Zeb for nuttin'. We is friends. Fact, right now I'm yore only friend. Nobody here seems to like you no more. No offense." Zeb focused intensely on his whittling.

Stephanie closed her eyes against his words. "But why?"

"I reckon it's 'cause you been makin' trouble fer us." He pulled off a long sliver of wood with his knife. "Well, since you been sick, you always sayin' somethin' to bring the man down on us. You 'member when Joshua hit you in the haid? He come to my house and do some more damage, then he keeps on 'til he wuz satisfied and tired. My mama is powerful mad at you."

Embarrassed, Stephanie clasped her hands over her mouth. "I'm sorry!"

"Yeah, but sorry don't hep none right now."

"I didn't know."

He pulled off another long sliver with his knife. "See, I is yore friend, so umma tel' ya 'bout yoreself." He winked. "Since you been feelin' betta, you ain't done nuttin' but sit around talkin' crazy."

Stephanie's Emerald Fever

Appalled by his accusations, Stephanie announced, "But, I washed the clothes."

"Gal, that ain't bout nuttin'. Sam been washin' them clothes by huh'self since she wuz brung here. You jest fills up the pot and makes the fire. You ain't heppin' Sam."

Zeb pulled off another sliver and tossed it into the fire. "You done sassed Old Jacob. Old Jacob!" He stopped whittling and looked Stephanie in the eye. "Old Jacob makes it a li'l easier on us. When things go wrong, Old Jacob covers fer us. He makes it right with Massa Andrews. Don't you understand?"

"Sam ain't got but a li'l taste of hair on her haid; darn ifn you ain't 'bout to make 'er pull it all out!" He paused briefly. "Folks round here say you act like you is a Andrews through and through. And that ain't good."

Stephanie began feeling flushed. She shook her head as if to deny the charges brought against her. From the sting of accusations Stephanie wriggled about. She could hardly keep still on the old stump.

"Mama Bell had to git you outta the Big House, 'cause you done forgit yoreself. She say you wuz all in Missy Andrews's face tryin' to talk. Gal, Missy Andrews don't know you! And jest 'cause she gave you ah teacake don't mean nuttin'. She gives all us slave cheerins them old stale teacakes. She too stingy to throw 'em out. You ain't nuttin' special 'round here!" Zeb's voice elevated then softened.

Gazing into the fire, Zeb sat quietly for a moment. "Mama Bell shudda beat you down. Yore mama had to do yore share of the work 'cause Massa Andrews said he didn't care ifn you wuz sick or not, long as that work of yourn got did. She tried to do yore share of the work, but she couldn't keep up. Yore po mama ain't tol' you 'bout that whippin', huh?"

Stephanie froze with fright. With her eyes locked on Zeb, she shamefully shook her head. Zeb shrugged. "See you gotta thank like Massa Andrews. He feel you done cheat him outta days work and he don't take too kindly to that."

Zeb exhaled and winced. Staring back into the fire, he shook his head remorsefully. Whispering softly he revealed, "They say she didn't even hollar none. She's one strong woman. Every time Old Man Andrews' whip came down on her po back, they say she just moaned a li'l." Gasping loudly, Stephanie instinctively grasped her shoulder, massaging it sympathetically. "Now, I can't say I wouldna hollered-out myself."

Facing Stephanie squarely, he declared, "You ain't been nuthin' but trouble since you been ailin'." Zeb hauled off and spit on the fire, the sizzle as searing as his words. "Now yore mama won't tell you, but I will. Gal, Massa Andrews ain't nuttin' to fool wit. He ah business man and he owns us. We is like cattle to him! They give milk, meat and leather, and you ain't no betta in his eyesight. He'll have you sole 'fore mornin' ifn you ain't careful."

Stephanie's Emerald Fever

Zeb was sorely blunt. Stephanie's brown eyes shifted wildly. She searched Zeb's face for a fraction of humor; only to find there was none. Her breath came in short pants. Surely her heart would burst with the agony of this revelation. Stephanie wriggled on her seat, heavy with disbelief. How dare he accuse her of being defiant? How could they possibly hate her when she was only being herself? It had to be a vicious lie!

As Zeb's words became real to Stephanie, a petrifying feeling made her spring to her feet. Turning sharply, her bare feet thudded swiftly in the moist dirt. Running blindly through the dark Stephanie tripped over stumps and rocks, bruising the skin against her ankle. Bleeding and anguished, Stephanie hobbled home, snuggled into her familiar bed tic and cried herself to sleep.

L.J. Maxie

Chapter Eight

But I Love Shopping

It was possible for an auctioned slave to get a decent home. Then again, most likely she wouldn't.

Chapter Eight

By morning, Stephanie realized what she had done. Refusing her share of the work, she had caused the entire quarters to suffer, especially M'dere. She wondered why Madge stayed with the Andrews family if they had treated her clan so badly. Gazing at the unfinished planks in the ceiling, Stephanie noticed that it had begun to rain. The plip and platter splashed down upon her and she squealed.

Quickly, M'dere emerged from behind the quilt. "What is it, Steffy?" Stephanie pointed to the enormous wet spot on the tic. "I meant to move this here tic last night. I knew it wuz gonna rain." She grabbed the corner of the tic and started to pull. "I feels sorry for folks wit jest dirt floors. It makes ah awful mess when it rains," M'dere rambled.

Stephanie could not help but look sorrowfully at M'dere. "Is it true?"

"Is what true?" M'dere asked, pulling a sleeping Sam along with the old tic.

"Did Old Man Andrews beat you because I didn't work the north field yesterday?"

"Who tol' you that?" she stalled, settling the tic in a new location.

"It doesn't matter." She wrung her hands. "Did he strike you or not?" she persisted.

M'dere smiled. "Oh, he hit me a few times, but it weren't bad."

Stephanie folded her arms and shuffled her feet, as reality weighed on her conscience. "Why didn't you tell me?"

"Well, some thangs cheerins shouldn't worry 'bout." She raised the old blanket and moved the wet spot toward the bottom of the tic.

"Why didn't you tell me I've broken all the rules around this place?"

M'dere sighed. "You wuz sick, child. And I thought people would be tolerant wit you. I guess, I wuz wrong." M'dere walked toward the kitchen area to finish making breakfast. When she turned her back, Stephanie noticed that the back of her blouse was soiled with dried blood stains.

Wincing inside, she cast her gaze shamefully to the floor. "I didn't mean to cause this family any harm," she admitted. "It's a loving family. You love Sam and she loves you." Walking over to the table, Stephanie pulled out a chair. "I'm learning a lot," she nodded. "Some of the characters around here are hilarious."

Stephanie's voice softened. "I know that more than eight people are forced to live in a one room house. Even though they don't know each other at first, it's still like one big family.

They count on each other. Uncle June Bug is really nobody's uncle. He has no idea where his family is, but he treats everyone with love and respect. He's a good man.

"And Old Jacob," she added. "Everyone in the quarters honors him. They depend on him although he's funny and says things to keep you laughing.

"When you work and live in a place like this, you've got to find something to laugh about. Although Mama Bell hit me, she meant me no harm. She was just trying to spare me a horrible fate. I understand all of this now. And starting today, I'm going to carry my own load."

Tears filled M'dere's eyes. She reached out to hold her firstborn. "I knows, Baby Gal, I knows. You is havin' a hard time wit dis here sickness."

With new jubilation, Stephanie got on with her morning. She was going to work in the field today. Even without sunscreen protection, Stephanie was determined to show everyone that she was one of the best field workers ever. The statement she made to Madge about slaves being made to show respect haunted her. Secretly, she asked for forgiveness. As the day waned, Stephanie fervently went about her work in the field.

The following morning came quickly. Her body ached with every movement she made. Sitting before the fireplace, she nursed scrapes and bruises earned from the hard labor in the field. She pushed the aches aside, determined that she would pull her share of the work.

It was hardly dawn when Stephanie ate her biscuit and peach preserves. Dressed in her cotton shift, she sat at the table and waited for Uncle June Bug to bring the wagon around. The whinny of a horse from the direction of the big house drew her interest. Peering out the window, Stephanie discovered their early visitor was the man on the horse, Joshua, an overseer she had grown to loathe just as much as the other slaves. What could he possibly want this early in the morning?

Remembering her unpleasant encounter with Joshua, Stephanie shied away from the window then bolted for M'dere's area of the room. To give M'dere a little privacy an old quilt hung from the ceiling to divide the room. Behind the quilt M'dere sat on her tic combing her hair. She was reaching for her kerchief when the expression on Stephanie's face stopped her short, revealing that something was wrong.

Joshua pulled his horse right up to the porch, tied it to a post then stepped upon the rickety porch. The thump and clink of his boots against the old wooden boards made them search each other's eyes with nervous concern. Without so much as a gentle knock, Joshua burst inside their home, his muddy boots tracking the floor. "Whar is that gal? I saw 'er from the winda!"

Stephanie hid behind the makeshift room divider while M'dere faced Joshua. "Yas, Sah, you did. What you want wit 'er?"

Joshua grinned. Pushing back his hat, he revealed murky eyes that testified of late night drinking. "That's all I needs to know."

As quickly as Joshua arrived, he left. From inside the house, the thump and clink of heavy boots walked out the door and back across the small porch. Unexpectedly, he leaped to the ground, got on his horse, and rode away.

Stephanie slowly emerged from behind M'dere's room divider. "What was that all about?"

"I don't know," M'dere said, removing the hanging quilt. "But ah gots a sneaky suspicion."

No sooner had M'dere finished her words another thud hit the porch. The door flew open. In the foggy dawn, Zeb stood panting. With terrified eyes, he heralded, "Did ya hear?" he asked breathlessly. "Lordy, theys gonna take Miss Steffy to the sell tomorrow!"

Visibly upset, M'dere allowed the quilt to fall absently to the floor. With trembling hands she nervously reached for

Stephanie, her firstborn. All of the commotion had awakened Sam and she burst into tears. Walking as if his feet were concrete blocks, Zeb finally made his way toward the two. Sorrowfully shaking his head, he placed his arms around the both of them. "You didn't deserve this kinda fate, Miss Steffy. You really is a good person." With hat in hand, he hung his head and sauntered out of the door.

Stephanie was confused. She loved a good bargain, but somehow this kind of sale didn't feel right. Also, why was everyone crying just because she was going shopping? Then it dawned on her. They would sell *her* tomorrow!

Her legs felt too flimsy to support her weight. Stunned, her body slid under M'dere's protective grasp, slipping into a crumpled heap on the floor. "They are going to sell *me*? How can this be possible? You can't sell another human. It's, like, immoral!"

There was no way Stephanie was going to stand still and let them sell her. M'dere was in severe mourning so there was no use consulting with her. Stephanie had to think fast. What could she do? Where could she hide?

She could imagine herself standing on the selling block with potential buyers opening her mouth to check her teeth. Stephanie paced the floor. "No way I'm going through that kind of humiliation," she vowed.

Stephanie's Emerald Fever

Walking toward the window, Stephanie nervously cast her eyes toward the big house. Through the morning darkness she saw a glimmer of light. This light usually meant the servants were stirring and making preparations for the day. Focusing on the light, her mind wandered back to a discussion she'd overheard around the fire. The elder slaves talked of their experiences on the selling block. She heard how they raised their dresses to check their legs, as if buying a horse. And they would examine the soles of their feet to see if they were lame or injured. "No way!" she exclaimed loudly. "No freakin' way!"

Suddenly, a plan came together in Stephanie's bewildered head. She would ride the wagon to the north field like usual, work throughout the day then run away when it was time to load up for home. She would carry a small bag of food and escape just like Old Jacob. Unlike Old Jacob though, her escape plan was to be successful. Although she was scared, fear fueled her brilliant plan.

After Stephanie carefully planned her escape, she sought nourishment for her journey. Selecting two large biscuits, she placed a little dry salt bacon between them. Even though she loved M'dere's peach preserves, she learned that the syrupy sweetness would attract ants and other pests. Dry biscuits would be best.

Stephanie had watched M'dere wrap biscuits in a cloth to carry to the field so she copied M'dere's wrapping technique. With her biscuits securely swaddled, she placed them on the table. Rushing to the water bucket, Stephanie picked up her personal drinking jar which rested on a cloth beside the bucket. Picking up an old dipper, she carefully measured the water as it filled the jar. When the jar was full Stephanie tightened the lid securely. Placing the biscuits on top of the jar, she tied the kerchief gently around them, recognizing that biscuits would crumble easily.

Working as fast as she could, Stephanie put on M'dere's dress as well as her good work shoes. M'dere's dress had more cloth; therefore it would give more protection in the woods than her simple cotton shift. Since Mrs. Sadie had not finished the moccasins, M'dere's shoes would be needed for running through the tall grass and dense brush.

In her heart, M'dere knew that Stephanie was plotting to run away. Not knowing which fate would be worse, she didn't speak a word. It was possible for an auctioned slave to get a decent home; then again, most likely she wouldn't.

Stephanie tried to recall the song Old Jacob sang, "Follow the Drinking Gourd." She had heard that freedom was at the end of the drinking gourd but what exactly was a drinking gourd, and where was it?

Stephanie examined the kerchief she'd tied around her food. Although her bloodline was that of a stubborn Andrews', being a slave made her apprehensive and immovable in her quest for freedom. There was no way she was going to be sold from her surrogate family. Stephanie made preparations and mumbled to herself. "Think, Stephanie. When was slavery abolished?" But, try as she might, she was unable to extract the data from her mangled memory. Now she wished she had paid more attention in history class. At the time, other things seemed more important. If she could just remember, perhaps she would not have to run away at all. Horrified, she did recall that even after slavery was abolished, some states continued to keep their slaves or paid them very low wages.

It was still dark out when the field wagon arrived. Stephanie waited anxiously on the front porch. Hearing the clamor from the horse-drawn wagon she prepared to leave. With an unbalanced grinding sound, the squeaky wagon rolled right up to the porch and stopped. Holding the reins in one hand Uncle June Bug tipped his hat nodding Stephanie a good morning. Like a lady, she nodded back. Raising her oversized dress she climbed aboard, being careful not to step on the spare fabric she felt dresses didn't necessarily need.

M'dere walked slowly out the door. Quietly, she pulled the leather strap door handle and yanked it tightly. Without looking at the people seated inside, M'dere boarded the wagon and sat on the seat beside Unka June Bug. Stephanie knew that M'dere held her lips tightly when worried; right now she wished she could comfort her. Although everyone in the wagon was silent, Stephanie was sure they had heard the distressing news.

The wagon wobbled along in the brisk morning breeze. Desperately clenching her overstuffed kerchief, Stephanie tried not to look suspicious. Foretelling her escape plan, the water made a splashing sound when Unka June Bug would hit a bump on the unpaved road. Her heartbeat was so rapid she could actually see her clothing rising and falling beneath her chin.

Mrs. Sadie was seated beside Stephanie. She reached out and gave her arm a loving squeeze. Looking toward the star filled sky; Mrs. Sadie slowly closed her eyes and nodded her kerchief-wrapped head. Stephanie had no idea what she meant with that nod, but she had ideas of her own.

Stephanie worked hard that day. With a small knife, she cut cucumbers and gathered them in her skirt. Every minute she was hoping someone would tell her the sell was off. Stephanie promised herself she would not make any more trouble. She was going to be a good worker.

As Stephanie toiled, the sun finally stood high in the sky. She wiped sweat from her brow with the back of her hand. The huge dress was tremendously hot, but she would need the extra fabric for protection.

Across the field, Zeb was working particularly hard. Sweat ran down the tips of his curly red hair. From time to time, he pulled off his hat to mop his tanned forehead. He was more than pleasing to her eyes. His green eyes suggested he was of mixed decent. Squinting in the sun, Stephanie realized how much Zeb looked like the guy she'd met at the mall. Their resemblance was uncanny. She shook her head to remove the absurd suggestion. However, Stephanie smiled to herself, and wondered if she'd ever see Zeb again.

While Stephanie picked the dirty, prickly cucumbers she reminded herself that Zeb lived up to the name, 'Honest Zeb.' He had not lied to her and she appreciated that quality in him. Him calling her a 'Brat' to her face was exactly what she needed to hear. Unfortunately, it was too late to make amends for her ghastly behavior.

When it was time to eat lunch Stephanie only nibbled a bite of the two biscuits. She had to save the bread for her trip to the north. After lunch, Mrs. Sadie worked the row of cucumbers beside Stephanie. Until now, she had not noticed that Mrs. Sadie's bottom lip turned upwards like a fish. This facial quirk caused her upper lip to follow suit. She also had extremely round eyes and a small nose. Stephanie realized she would never forget Mrs. Sadie's fish-like features.

Old Jacob once told Sam that all of Mrs. Sadie's children had been sold. That was her reason for being strict on misbehaving children, she felt that a good child was valuable to their Master and would not be sold. All four of Mrs. Sadie's children had been sold one by one, with the last child being snatched right from her breast. From every account, Mrs. Sadie had a good reason to look like a sad old cod fish. Her arms were empty and her house…quiet.

As evening fell, Stephanie became antsy. She now knew which trail to take for her escape. From the long side of the wagon, Joshua would not be able to see her duck into the brush. It was possible for the workers on the wagon to cover for her then no one would discover her escape until morning. If her absence was undiscovered during the evening count, morning would bring plenty of time for a head start. However, traveling on foot would make Stephanie's journey slow and laborious, her capture would be almost certain. How she prayed for the elements to aid her in her quest home.

Chapter Nine

Whew! What is That Smell?

How she hoped for a stray doggie or even a cute little raccoon.

Chapter Nine

Stephanie walked alongside the wagon with her provisions tucked under her arm. Blossoming Dogwood trees and thick brambles called to her. "It's time to go." Waving frantically, they whispered that her time had come. Stephanie lifted her eyes to the top of the swaying Cottonwood trees. Her eyes danced from limb to limb while the birds wept, "Will her now! Will her now!" Even the strong thick roots beckoned her with promises of freedom.

Stephanie looked at M'dere who was riding inside the wagon. She held her head high and refused to acknowledge Stephanie. Joshua looked away then rode his horse to the front of the dusty trail.

With a tight knot in her stomach, Stephanie crouched as if stopping to pick up something then she crept alongside the wagon. When she neared the trail, she ducked out of sight and ran. In Stephanie's haste the 'kerchief around her hair became entangled on a limb. Waving in the breeze, the 'kerchief was a signal to anyone who saw it.

The infrequently used trail guided her through the dense woods. The unfamiliar scents of nameless trees wrapped themselves around her face like an invisible veil, forcing her to breathe their bitter odors. Behaving rudely, thorny bushes tore at her dress and ripped out her hair. As if punishing her for escaping, hundreds of tiny twigs pricked her skin as she barreled through the tall weeds.

Stephanie paused long enough to pull the large dress around her waist so her legs could run even faster. "Sweet Freedom, Sweet Freedom," she puffed. "Sweet Freedom."

In her mind, she could not imagine selling another living being, ever, ever! Sweat ran down her legs. How they ached under the nervous strain her freedom demanded. Because Stephanie was wearing oversized shoes blisters began introducing themselves to her tender heels, but still she ran. She was going to run until she collapsed.

The smiling faces of her mom and dad hung teasingly over her head. She could see the hurtful expression on Madge's face when she said those harmful things. The old painting of Master Andrews in her father's study made her question the integrity of the Andrews' name. How could Old Man Andrews raise his hand against M'dere for lost production? Furthermore, how could he raise his hand against anyone?

As Stephanie ran, she recalled Sam giving her the grand tour of the slave quarters. When they gathered clothing to wash, Sam showed Stephanie the place where disobedient slaves were beaten. Sam felt that if Stephanie saw the 'beating shed' it would remind her to be obedient.

Old Man Andrews had a special place built just for the purpose of punishing slaves. Disobedient slaves were tied to the side of the barn with arms and legs spread apart. The slaves naked backs were exposed to deliver what they felt would be the most effective beating. Stephanie could visualize the old man having M'dere tied to the side of the barn and beating her with a whip until his heart was contented. Tears plumped in her eyes, now she understood what it was like to want freedom more than anything else.

Stephanie had to stop running. With distance between her and the plantation she felt a little safer. Taking off her mother's clunky shoes, she laced them together then tossed them over her shoulder. Cautiously searching the ground and trees, she watched for snakes and other small animals. Being alone in the woods made her nervous. Her panic-stricken body begged her to run a while longer. It was still light and resting was an option, but keeping her toes was not. No, she didn't want to lose her toes like, Old Jacob.

It was late evening when Stephanie noticed that a thick grove of trees had stolen the fading sunlight. Her eyes explored the grayish mesh that seemed to cover her way. Suddenly, a shadowy dampness fell around her. Stephanie held out her hand feeling the cool mist in her palm. Gradually, the trail became damp, musky, and smelled of mold. As she walked along, the air that sustained her became foul. Gasping for breath Stephanie used her hand to cover her nose while holding her provisions in the other. The stench was horrible and not easily filtered.

Slowing her pace, Stephanie's eyes absently searched tangled trees and gnarled bushes for the source of the unpleasant smell. Suddenly, a low grunting sound vibrated in her ear. Frowning, Stephanie stopped walking and listened. She could tell that the sound was coming from behind her. How she hoped for a stray doggie or even a cute little raccoon. Feeling that it was neither, an eerie feeling overtook her. Wide-eyed, Stephanie continued her investigation in sheer terror, something or someone was there. Slowly turning on her heels, Stephanie strained to hear once more. She heard nothing but the strong pants of her own breath. Although the woods appeared calm, Stephanie's senses told her that something was dreadfully amiss.

Agitated birds suddenly exploded from the tops of trees as if shot from cannons. The unexpected noise made Stephanie cower with fear. Seeing feathers, twigs, and leaves falling around her, she glanced upward. She soon realized that this debris was falling as a result of the bird's rapid departure. With stillness in the air, she could hear the ragged breathing of something biding its time. All of her senses told her that danger was present. In response to her body's warning the hair on her neck stood on end.

Preparing to run, Stephanie tucked her supplies under her arm. Hurriedly, she unlaced the shoes then tossed them to the ground. Shoving her feet securely inside, she quickly tied the laces. Stephanie felt threatened by the unseen danger that lurked in the bushes. What could she do? Because the cucumber knives were carefully counted, Stephanie had no weapon to defend herself. And even if she had stolen a cucumber knife she doubted she owned the courage to harm anything.

The grunting grew more pronounced then Stephanie heard a rustling sound. She saw the bushes part to allow something swift passage. With a horrifying squeal, a shadowy black animal stopped at the edge of the bushes. It was a sort of hog but tusks protruded from both sides of its mouth. Its skin was leathery and short sparse hair covered its entire body. Staring into the animal's crusty black eyes, Stephanie backed up in disbelief. Much to her regret, the animal already had her in its sights.

With a lowered head, the beast followed Stephanie's slightest movement. Every nerve in her body told her that the beast was preparing to charge. Her heart was already spent from her exhausting journey but now it had to work double time to fuel her tired body. Both knees jerked with tremors at the sight of the beast, her thighs twitched, anticipating her next move.

Dare she run? Would the animal overtake and kill her? No one would ever find her remains in these woods. A shudder ran through Stephanie's body at the thought of being mangled by a wild beast. With muscles contracting violently, Stephanie decided she could not allow the creature to take her life. Adrenaline gave strength to her limbs and she bolted through the dense, dank woods.

Stephanie's Emerald Fever

The beast snorted while its prey ran hysterically through the woods. Displaying its power, the beast tossed its head and expelled a ferocious high pitched squeal. The strident sound pierced the musky air. Although Stephanie was running with all her might, she heard the heavy animal as it gave chase with a thunderous trot.

Because Stephanie was not watchful a low hanging branch whipped her, gashing her forehead. Putting her forearm before her face, Stephanie hid herself from the rest of the branches that slapped against her skin. Although she tried desperately to outrun the animal she felt the heat of the animal's rancid breath upon her heels.

With aching legs Stephanie recognized that her frail body was no match for the four-legged beast. Feeling as though her heart would stop, Stephanie realized the animal was too swift. Although she had gained a little distance Stephanie realized there was no way to keep up the strenuous demands. With a prayer in her heart she prepared to surrender herself to the creature.

Stephanie stopped abruptly. She turned to face her repulsive stalker. Tossing her provisions aside, her fists became tight knots. "Come and get me!" she panted, "I can't run anymore!" The beast stopped running and snorted. Its short, naked tail flicked back and forth menacingly while its crusty black eyes were fixed on Stephanie. Simultaneously, she knew she had become an easy prey for the beast.

Breathing raggedly, she locked her legs and closed her eyes tightly. Stephanie grew frustrated. "Come on!" she yelled again, her voice echoing loudly throughout the hollowed grove. "What are you waiting for?" she strained. "This life is not worth living anyway!" Timidly, she opened one eye to monitor the animal. "Come on!" she yelled pacing back and forth in a nervous swagger. "I'd rather be dead than be a slave!" Stephanie felt her emotions erupting from inside and she burst into tears. Closing her fist tightly, she was almost prepared to fight. "Take me out of my misery now!" she sobbed.

Stephanie paced upon the damp ground with aching feet. Her skin was raw with abrasions from the lashing of the spiteful trees. Seemed her head would burst from the anticipation of an obvious death. Stephanie blasted. "Do you hear me, you Jurassic reject? I said I can't take this anymore!" she cried. Covering her eyes, she screamed. "Just do it!"

All of a sudden, Stephanie heard the thunderous sound of the hooves coming toward her faster and faster. She peered though her fingers. The animal snorted and gained speed. Drawing herself into a tight ball she trembled and waited for her end.

Unexpectedly, the sound of the hooves stopped with a loud thump then there was silence. In the sudden stillness, the haunting cry of a large bird was heard overhead.

Stephanie's Emerald Fever

Stephanie gradually removed her hands from her eyes. She felt herself, noticing that she was still alive. Although, it was getting dark she could see that only a few feet away the beast lay dead in its tracks. Standing above it was Zeb.

"Zeb!" Stephanie screamed to the top of her lungs. "Oh Zeb! Zeb! I'm glad to see you." Trying to catch her breath she wheezed. "This thing was about to eat me!"

Zeb proudly inflated his chest, his breathing loud and irregular. In his fist he clenched a bloody hunting knife. "I been behind you a long time, Miss Steffy," he puffed. "I saw the wild hog—"

"Wild hog?" Stephanie cringed.

Zeb nodded breathless. "It wuz a wild hog." He wiped sweat from his brow with his forearm. "There's lots of 'um in these parts. You is lucky. Mostly, they run in packs."

"Packs! You mean there are more!"

"Yep." He pointed to the still animal. "That one is kinda young," he rasped.

"But it's huge!" Stephanie gazed down on the bleeding monster. "And it smells awful!" She held her hand over her nose.

Zeb nodded, pulling Stephanie away from the terrible sight.

Zeb ushered Stephanie into his arms. Now, his face was familiar to her, his tender touch was not, even so she welcomed the hearty embrace.

Using his handkerchief, Zeb nursed the laceration on Stephanie's forehead. She stood quietly and relished his attention.

Stephanie was still breathing loudly. She placed her hand nervously atop Zeb's while he applied pressure to her wound. With the other hand she held her trembling heart. They shared an uneasy laugh between them. "I was so scared. I was preparing to die, like, right now!"

Zeb became serious, "Miss Steffy, the time is right."

Focusing on Zeb's shapely lips, Stephanie frowned. "What are you talking about?" She gazed around the wooded area trying to find something right about the situation. "What's right?"
"Fer us," Zeb admitted.

"Us?" Both Stephanie's brows shot up at once.

"To run away together!" Zeb put away his 'kerchief and placed both arms around Stephanie's waist.

"What?" Stephanie placed her hands against his and pushed them from their unwanted resting place.

"Don't say you don't 'member." He stroked her brown cheek, daring her to look away with the sincerity in his eyes.

Stephanie questioned. "We were going to run away together?"

Zeb nodded, "Massa Andrews jest made it come sooner than we boff spected."

Searching his green eyes, Stephanie scowled, "I can't believe this."

Zeb held his body closer to Stephanie, forcing her against a large Sweet Gum tree. "Don't say that, Miss Steffy. Our dream is coming true," he whispered, lightly kissing her forehead.

Stephanie tried to move from Zeb's grasp. "We were, like, going to run away to freedom?"

"Un huh," Zeb sighed with a soft kiss to the cheek. "Then we is gonna jump the broom," he said softly.

Focusing on his mouth, Stephanie repeated, "We are going to jump what?"

"The broom. That fever done made you forgit. You done forgit what we means to each other, ain't you?"

Stephanie stammered, "Zeb — I —"

"I knowed it," Zeb receded. "I could see it in yore face 'round the fire. You act lack you don't even know me none."

Stephanie's voice became soft, compassion replaced fear. "I guess I forgot, Zeb."

"That don't change things none...the fever, I mean. I still loves you. I've always loved you, from the moment they brung you to Massa Andrews' plantation."

"I'm sorry," she stuttered. "I guess the fever erased my memory."

"Erased yore memory," he said tenderly. "Well, I guess some memories need erasin'."

Zeb reminisced. "I think back and it seem like it wuz yesterday when I saw you git ofen' that wagon. I ain't never saw anything lack you. You wasa sked li'l ole thang. You didn't speak no Anglish. But them big brown eyes spoke fer you. I wanted to protect you from that moment on."

Stephanie blushed.

"It was them brown eyes that told me how you felt 'bout me. 'Fore yore papa left, he told me to take care of you."

"My papa!"

"Un huh. I laughed, he didn't hafta ask me to take care of you. Anyways, I promised him I would. Marryin' you is the most natural thang to do."

"Zeb. I'm only sixteen," she admitted timidly.

"And I'm seventeen. You is almost past the right age to marry."

"Past the age to marry?"

"We is going to the norf. Whereas we kin be free. We's gonna leave all this behind us and start a family."

"A family?" Stephanie's eyes widened. "We're, like, going to have babies?" she grimaced.

Zeb's eyes narrowed as he smiled. "Now we done talked 'bout that, too. We is gonna have lots of cheerins."

'Cheerins?' she repeated with a glare.

"We can git a head start right now ifn' you want." He tenderly brushed her cheek.

"A head start?" Stephanie cocked her head to one side, unsure of what she heard.

Making cheerins." He grinned. "And Old Man Andrews won't make no profit offen our cheerins 'cause he ain't gonna git 'em."

"Come on, Zeb," Stephanie pleaded doubtfully. "What would Old Man Andrews do with children?"

Zeb cringed. "I tol' you we is like cattle to him. Good breedin' stock means mo money."

Stephanie placed her hands to her flushed cheeks. "He sells them!" Horror emerged in her eyes. "He actually sells children!"

Embarrassed, Zeb shrugged. "It's painful to remember, huh? Well he ain't gonna git our cheerins," he declared forcefully.

"I can't have children, Zeb."

"If you is tryin' ta say you is barren, it don't madder, Miss Steffy."

Stephanie gave him a serious shove. "No!" she confessed. "I'm, like," she winced, "too young."

"Well, we can wait. But, you is in your prime right now for havin' yungns."

"I'm sorry, Zeb," she whined. "But I've got to make a career for myself before marriage."

"Ca wreer?" Zeb shook his head and shrugged. "You can learn that after we gits married. Ain't never known a woman who wanted to make cart wheels, but ifn' that's what you want to do, then…"

Stephanie's Emerald Fever

Stephanie burst into laughter. She reached out to comfort Zeb. Looking into his mesmerizing green eyes she admitted, "Zeb. You are, like, *so* hot. You have the most incredible eyes I have ever seen. If I was at home, my friends would be totally jealous. Any girl would be proud to be with you. It's just that," she paused and cast her gazed toward the ground, "there are some things you don't understand about me."

"I know you is ailin'," he whispered. "But I'll stand by you 'til you gits betta. It don't change how I feel none. I can't deny what I feels inside me, Miss Steffy. I have a powerful hankerin' to be wit you."

Stephanie thought for a moment. What would her life be like if she never returned home? If what she was experiencing was real, she needed to start her life somewhere. "What's going to happen when they find out you're, like, gone? They really depend on you and they'll notice when you don't show up."

Zeb shook his head. "I' ain't worried 'bout that right now.

I feels free. I ain't never knowd what freedom feels like. Since I wuz young, all I ever knowd is that there plantation. I had a feelin' there's mo to life than that plantation back there. I wants a real wife. I wants to be married by a real preacher, like Unka June Bug. I wants a home of my own, not lack them rotten old sticks we lives in."

Stephanie became teary. "I don't blame you, Zeb. Life is far grander than what you will ever know."

"Whoa now." He looked into Stephanie's eyes through the moonlight. "Do I see tears?" He held her tightly, stroking her back with loving glides. "It's okay. We is together now."

Stephanie smiled weakly. Through her tears she said, "Yes, we are."

Zeb became quiet. He gazed into Stephanie's large, cat-like eyes. Warmth crept over him.

Stephanie shyly blinked her eyes. Her mind was torn between the present and the future. Studying the moonlight in his eyes, she thought, 'Zeb is totally gorgeous and he wants me! Why couldn't we have been born during the same time?'

Staring into Stephanie's eyes, Zeb quietly placed his palm behind her head. Simultaneously he pulled her toward him in an effort to kiss her.

At first, Stephanie was shy but looking into the longing eyes of Zeb, there was no way she could deny what she was also feeling. She parted her lips and placed them against the warmth of Zeb's shapely lips. Instantly, a moist heat arose between them and their embrace tightened with the tension of the moment.

Stephanie felt her insides heave and flutter away. As if lying in her own comfortable bed, she floated on the comfort of Zeb's embrace, reeling with a hunger for him to hold her tighter.

Separating from the kiss, Zeb searched her eyes. "Tell me that you don't love me none. Your kiss is the same as it always was. Only, the thangs goin' on 'round us makes it betta."

Turning her back toward Zeb, Stephanie requested, "Zeb. We can't jump the broom. You must go home. If you love me like you say you do then please go home."

"I can't do that, Miss Steffy. This here is our dream. I can't give it up lack that." Zeb's expression became serious. "I've already taken the chance to be wit you. Don't jest send me away."

"I can't explain it to you, Zeb. It's too complicated. Please trust my judgment and go back. Go back before they start looking for you."

"You ain't makin' a lick of sense. You said you loved me."

"I do, that's why I know you must return home. This is something I must do alone. Do you understand me? I must…do this…alone!"

"Miss Steffy, I can't leave you. It don't feel right. A piece of me feels empty inside." Zeb's voice grew softer, his voice pleaded, "I don't lack that feelin', Miss Steffy. Don't send me aw—"

"Zeb!" she shouted, looking painfully into his rejected eyes. "Listen to me. You can't go where I'm going."

Zeb turned his back. "It's dark now. How you gonna make it witout me? You saw what could happen—like that wild hog over there!"

"I can't lie, Zeb. I'm, like, scared out of my wits. But I'm not as scared for me..." her voice began to tremble, "...as I am for you."

Zeb's voice became cold. "I know what this is 'bout. This 'bout my paw ain't it?"

Stephanie became numb. She shook her head. "You mean—because your dad is white?"

Zeb turned away from Stephanie's sigh. "I knowd it. You sked I'm gonna be lack my paw, ain't you?" He turned to face her. "Well I ain't nuttin' like *Joshua!*" he blasted.

"Joshua, the overseer?" she questioned, making distance between them.

"You said it didn't madder at first!" Zeb begged. "Please don't change yore mind now."

Shaking her head in disbelief, Stephanie's emotions became a jumbled mass of confusion. She knew she needed to console Zeb. Part of her conscience wanted to hate Zeb but the other part felt intense sorrow. "No, Zeb. You'll never be like your father." She lifted his chin and looked into his eyes. "Zeb."

Shamefully he turned his gaze from Stephanie's view. "Zeb. Look at me—I promise I'll come back for you, okay?"

Zeb was plainly disappointed. He removed Stephanie's hand and held it. "You is kind. I understand you is jest sayin' that. I ain't never gonna see you no mo, Miss Steffy." Disillusioned, he turned his stare toward the ground. "Being bone of Joshua is lacka curse I can't gita way from."

Suddenly, Zeb looked up. Fighting back tears he held Stephanie by the shoulders and urgently shook her. "You listen to me, Miss Steffy," he sniffled. "And you betta hear me good. Up the road a piece is a farm house. Now, ifn you can git there, they have a barn. You might be able to spend the night in the barn ifn you is quiet." Wiping a falling tear from his cheek Zeb ordered, "You be careful now. It ain't gonna be easy, so take God 'long wit you."

Zeb turned to face the darkness. He walked back down the small path. Kicking bushes aside with his feet Zeb searched for something. He picked up an object and walked up to Stephanie. Placing the object in her hands he sighed loudly and looked toward the sky. "Here," he gave her the supplies she had dropped earlier. "You dropped this.

"Now don't you fret 'bout me. Zeb will be alright. I'll make it back to the plantation a'fore mornin'." Zeb held Stephanie in his arms once more and kissed her. His bitter tears felt cool against her cheek. Reaching into his back pocket he retrieved Stephanie's lost 'kerchief.

"My 'kerchief! Where did I…"

Looking into Stephanie's bewildered eyes, Zeb sealed her lips with a final kiss. Then he placed two fingers across her lips. "Sh-sh," he whispered. "Be safe." Zeb kissed the scarf then tied it around his neck. "I'll be prayin' for ya, Miss Steffy." Having said those words, Zeb secured his knife in his sheath and disappeared into the darkness.

Stephanie's Emerald Fever

Chapter Ten

Oh, My Aching Legs!

"I'm from New York! And I'm not a slave!"

Chapter Ten

Stephanie placed her fingers against her lips and remembered the tingle of the passionate kiss. Her heart ached to think that Joshua was Zeb's father. How could something so vile produce something as inwardly beautiful as Zeb? There was no doubt in her mind that Joshua would put his own son on the selling block. Stephanie shuddered as she thought of Zeb standing bare chested on the selling block. She could visualize him with hands tied and feet bound; no doubt, he would bring an outrageously high price.

The moon gave light to the path before her. Although Zeb had possession of Stephanie's scarf, he did not take her fear with him. She stumbled along the overgrown path, fearful of what lie ahead.

Stephanie heard the barking of a dog just ahead and saw a small glimmer of light indicating the farm house was near. Wrapping her dress around her legs, she stopped walking and observed the house though the bushes. As Zeb had said, a rickety old farm house sat among a grove of trees. Dare she knock on the door? Perhaps the people inside would tell someone she was a runaway.

Almost holding her breath, Stephanie crouched and watched. The dog began barking wildly. Soon, a man carrying a rifle came outside on the porch. He was white-skinned and at least seven feet tall, in Stephanie's eyes.

The man gazed into the woods. "What is it boy, a coon? You see something out there?" He patted the dog's head. "You ain't never wrong." The man waited for a while, then went back inside the house.

The dog continued to bark. Stephanie knew that eventually the dog would come after her. The door opened again but this time the man and a small frail woman came out onto the porch. To project his voice, the man raised his hand to the side of his mouth. "Ifn you is out there, you is welcome to come inside!"

Stephanie remained as still as she could. Could the man actually mean what he was saying, or was it just a trick to get her to come out from hiding?

"I know you is out there!" he shouted. "We ain't gonna hurt you none!"

Stephanie wanted to believe him. She was tired, hungry, and bleeding. What did she have to lose? She held her 'kerchief of crushed biscuits and water over her head then slowly walked out of the brush. "Please, Sir. Don't shoot me. I'm not armed."

"Come on out here sos I can see you." The man squinted to see through the darkness.

"Yes, Sir. I'm coming."

Clad in only a nightgown, the man's wife stepped forward. "Well, she ain't no more than a child, Papa. She's a brave soul. Come on round here child. Is you hungry?" she inquired, tugging fretfully at her sheer gown. The man cautiously looked around the yard. Pushing Stephanie inside the house, he closed the door quickly behind them.

Looking Stephanie over, he stated his observations. "You is a scrawny little old thing, ain't you? Ain't hardly a mouthful for a starving bear." Putting the gun back on the rack, he lit another kerosene lamp.

Taking in her surroundings, Stephanie asked, "May I sit down for just a moment?" She sighed loudly as she made herself comfortable by sitting on a small wooden bench.

The man looked down at his wife. "Ma, she talk funny."

Remembering that she could not speak English very well, Stephanie started slowly. "Ah is tryin' to gits to freedom."

"Nope." The man leaned forward and pulled his pipe from beneath a wooden box. "That don't git it. I want you to talk like you did afore—when you asked to sit down." He sat down in his rocking chair and started to rock.

Surprised, Stephanie brightened. "You understood me?"

With his pipe clenched in his teeth, he gazed at his wife as he rocked. "Yep, and you sound a might funny. Where is you from?"

Swallowing hard she asked, "May I tell you the truth?"

"Of course," he said slowly. "We is here to hep."

"I'm from New York," she grinned. "There, I said it. I'm from New York." She yelled it louder with deliverance. "New York! And I'm not a slave. I'm free!"

"Yep, yore shore nuff is free, ifn you is from New York. But thare ain't no way they is gonna believe you...least, not in these parts. You better come wit me."

They led Stephanie to the barn. The intense stench of cow manure insulted her delicate nose. They showed her the ladder to the hayloft. "Now you sleep here 'til mornin'. Ma will bring you some vittles then you can be on yore way. We boff hafta go to work in the mornin'. See, we is what you call slaves too."

"What?"

"Yep. We gots seven more years to work for Old Man Waters then we will be free too. This land will be ourn, and we won't owe nobody nuttin'."

Pulling her dress above her knees, Stephanie started up the ladder. "Good Lord!" she commented. "They make slaves out of everyone around here."

The man blew smoke from his pipe. "Now, I'm gonna give you fair warnin'. Ifn they come lookin' fer ya, you is on yore own. I'll do a lot of things to hep people, but admittin' to harborin' runaway slaves ain't one of 'em. Sos, I ain't seen you, ya hear?"

"Yes, Sir, I understand," she acknowledged politely.

The straw in the hayloft was dry and scratchy. Stephanie was sure small bugs had made homes inside this nest of straw, but she was hardly sane enough to care if her bed had bugs or not. At first Stephanie leaned against the straw. Restlessly, she rolled over on her side placing her face against her crossed forearms.

As she nodded the cow below made a peculiar slobbering sound. Startled, Stephanie raised her head to investigate almost forgetting where she was. Simultaneously, an insect stung her on the calf. Absently, she slapped at the source of discomfort then vigorously scratched the irritated site. A sluggish stupor closed Stephanie's eyes while exhaustion slowly pulled her head back to its resting place. Memories of Zeb's visit in the woods made Stephanie sigh and that sigh preceded blissful rest.

Stephanie's Emerald Fever

Chapter Eleven

A Painful Past

"That's my daddy, not Neal's daddy!"

Chapter Eleven

As Stephanie turned over in the hay, she felt a dream mist falling upon her. Visualizing her old room, she smiled. There were colorful rows of her favorite dolls. Her games were stacked neatly on the shelf. Surely, her stuff animals missed her after all these years. The room still looked the same. When they moved to New York, she wondered why they left her favorite bedroom set behind.

Seeing a beautifully wrapped gift sitting on her bed, she smiled. "Birthday Party," she said aloud.

Then, Stephanie saw herself as a little girl, standing before a full length mirror. Swaying back and forth in stocking feet, she admired the poofy layers of petty coats under her pink party dress. She beamed as her mother fussed over her.

"But Mom, I don't want to go to Neal's dumb old birthday party," she complained, flicking a satin rose around her waistband.

Stephanie's mom knelt down to tie her sash. Her thick blonde braid fell over her shoulder and she swept it behind her. Admiring her daughter, her large blue eyes sparkled.

Stephanie's Emerald Fever

"Sweetheart, you look beautiful. Don't you want to help Neal celebrate his second birthday? I know you're a big girl. But, you're only five. You and Neal still have a lot in common. You'll have a lot of fun, I promise." She pulled a fallen curl out of Stephanie's face. "Here, let's put on your special white shoes," she said softly.

While Stephanie's mom ushered on her shoes, she continued to protest. "Mommy. I don't want to go."

"Sweetie, why? You'll really enjoy yourself once you get there," she said, buckling the right shoe. Tenderly, she placed Stephanie's foot back on the floor and picked up the other shoe.

Stephanie moped. "Neal will get all the gifts and I won't get anything."

"Stephanie, honey. Neal is your cousin. It's selfish to wish for gifts at *his* birthday party. Everyone should enjoy their *own* birthday."

As her mom was reaching for the other foot, Stephanie snatched it back. "Neal shouldn't have any more birthdays," Stephanie announced vehemently.

"Stephanie!" Her mom stood up and swept a stray strand of hair behind her ear. Looking at her daughter with disbelief she stammered, "I can't believe you're saying these things."

"But Mom, Neal's Mom hugs him all the time and she doesn't hug me." Stephanie's eyes grew wide with disappointment.

"That's probably because she knows you don't want her hugs." She shook her finger at Stephanie. "You did tell her to take her hands off you at our Thanksgiving dinner."

Stephanie twisted her satin rose and the threads started to fray. "That's because she didn't bring me a gift."

"Honey, it was Thanksgiving, not Christmas."

Toying with the loose rose, Stephanie announced, "Aunt Reta always brings me a gift."

"That's because Aunt Reta doesn't have children, Sweetheart. She loves to shower children with gifts."

Stephanie's mother picked up her pink hairbrush from the dresser. She started to brush Stephanie's curly blonde hair. Stubbornly, Stephanie snatched her head away. "I don't want you to brush my hair. I want Madge to brush it!"

Blowing with exasperation, Stephanie's mom put the brush back on the dresser. "Sweetheart, Madge is getting ready to go shopping. She will drop you off at the party then pick you up afterwards."

Pushing out her bottom lip Stephanie pouted. "No! I want Madge to stay with me — I want her to stay!"

Stephanie's Emerald Fever

"Stephanie, I need to finish my proposal, so Madge has to shop for the family today. Please don't be difficult."

"Mommy, what did I say?" Stephanie's expression froze into an angry scowl. "What did I say?"

"Honey!"

"If Madge won't go with me, I won't go!" She folded her arms and locked her stance.

Her mom scratched her head and pleaded, "Now, Stephanie. Madge can't sit there and wait for you while you're having fun."

"I don't care." Stephanie kicked off her shoe. It landed near the door. "I want her to stay so she can hold me, like Neal's mother holds him."

Arlene shook her head. "Put your shoe back on, we've talked about this before, Stephanie. Madge is not your personal toy. She is a fully grown woman."

"I want her to go!" In her stocking feet, Stephanie kicked the other shoe across the room

Aggravated, Arlene knitted her brow. "Stop that! Madge can't go with you this time."

When Madge finished putting up her hair, she stood in Stephanie's doorway and watched. Her dark brown eyes narrowed with authority. Sternly, she addressed Stephanie, "Stephanie Andrews, that's enough of that! Put your shoes on, right now!" Madge softened her voice. "I don't mind staying, Arlene. I'll just take Stephanie to the store with me afterwards. It's really okay."

Stephanie frowned at her mother. "See! I told you."

Arlene sighed. "Stephanie, you're such a stubborn child. You can't always have things your way. Madge must take care of errands for the house."

Stephanie started to cry. "I want her to go..." She threw herself upon her bed, crushing the lovely satin dress. "I won't go unless Madge goes too!"

Madge walked inside the room and sat on Stephanie's bed. "Sweetie, I'll go if you promise to be on your best behavior. You have wrecked a few parties with your selfish behavior. If you misbehave this time, this will be your last party. Do you understand?"

Stephanie wiped a tear and sat up, her stocking feet digging vengefully into the plush bed spread. "Okay," she whimpered. "I'll be good. You can't go with me wearing that dress. It looks tacky."

Stephanie's Emerald Fever

Madge reached down and grasped her casual dress, "Oh, I look tacky, huh?"

Stephanie didn't answer, she only stared at Madge. Unexpectedly, she got off the bed, retrieved the hairbrush from the dresser then handed it to Madge. "Madge, will you brush my hair. Mommy hurts my head."

Madge looked at Arlene. "Is that alright with you?"

Arlene threw up her hands. "Sure, why not. I'm only a door mat around here anyway."

Madge cringed. "Don't say that, honey. It isn't true."

Frustrated, Arlene wrung her hands. "It's her Dad's fault. He's spoiled her rotten."

Stephanie looked into the face of her worried mother. "I'm standing right here. I can hear you, you know."

Madge finished brushing Stephanie's hair. To keep Stephanie's long ringlets out of her face she pinned her hair behind her ears with jeweled clips. Giving Stephanie a doll, Madge demanded, "Sugar, play with this until I change clothes, okay."

"Okay," Stephanie agreed, cheerfully reaching for the doll.

"And don't get dirty, okay," she warned, shaking her finger.

"Okay." Stephanie sat on her bed and started to comb the dolls hair.

As Madge walked down the hallway toward her room Arlene followed. "Honestly Madge, I just don't know. I've tried everything I can think of to…" Madge's bedroom door closed; Stephanie disobeyed Madge immediately.

She followed the two adults down the hallway and stood outside Madge's door. Using her foot she pushed the door slightly open.

Arlene hoisted herself upon Madge's antique bed then fidgeted with her long braid. "I'm so tired, Madge. I don't know what to do with that child." She rolled over on her stomach; swinging her feet back and forth behind her.

Accustom to Arlene's girlish behavior, Madge went to her closet to find a decent dress to wear, something that was not, so *tacky*.

As Arlene gently swung her feet she confided in Madge. "See Madge, sometimes I feel like she's totally out of control. She doesn't do anything I ask of her."

Madge found a pink floral dress. She pulled it from the closet and checked for wrinkles. "Maybe it's time to put something on her bottom."

Arlene was stunned. "Her *bottom*! Madge, I couldn't!"

Madge turned sharply toward Arlene and declared, "Why, Arlene Andrews. A little spanking never hurt anyone. If you don't get control of her now, you'll regret it later."

"Madge, if I spank Stephanie, Stephen will have me committed. You know how he feels about her."

Madge smiled devilishly. "Then, spank him too. Do you want me to take care of his rusty bottom? I'm still pretty good, you know."

Arlene giggled. "Did you actually spank Stephen?"

"Why don't you ask him?" Madge placed the dress on the bed then went back to the closet to select a pair of shoes.

Arlene thought for a moment. "Well, you could have another talk with him about Stephanie's behavior."

With her back turned to Arlene, Madge stood still. "Dear, how you and Stephen decide to raise that child of yours is your business. However, I can give a few gentle suggestions."

Stephanie was standing in the doorway listening to the entire conversation. She snatched the rose from her dress and frowned. "Just let her try to spank me. She'll be sorry."

Neal's parents, Grace and Allen, needed a little time alone. Stress was pulling on their marriage, so they desperately needed a few days to rekindle their affections.

Uncle Stephen and Aunt Arlene understood their dilemma. They had Madge to depend on, so it was never difficult to find time alone.

Stephen volunteered to keep Neal for a few days. However, he did not discuss this unpleasant arrangement with his daughter, Stephanie. Somehow, they both felt everything would work out fine between them.

Everyone in the family knew Stephanie was jealous of Neal, but felt that eventually, she would get over that jealousy.

Wearing his old college football shirt, Stephen stood in the open doorway, holding Neal in his arms. His brown eyes danced with excitement at the thought of having a toddler around the house. Stephen nuzzled his clean shaven face against Neal's. "He will be fine, guys. Don't worry."

Allen reached up and examined his brother's curly brown hair. "I see you've sprouted a few gray hairs. I hope you won't be completely gray by the time we get back," he kidded.

"Allen is right, Honey." Arlene separated a few gray stands with her fingers. "You are getting gray, right there at the temples. I hadn't noticed before."

Stephen blushed. "It's not my fault, Allen. Just stay married as long as I have and you'll sprout a few, too. Now, you guys have yourselves a great time! You need this mini-vacation."

Neal's mother seemed apprehensive. "I'm so nervous about leaving him here. We've never been apart."

"Come on Grace," Allen said, pulling on his wife's arm. "If anything, Neal will be spoiled rotten when we get back."

Grace kissed Neal's tiny hand, and held it against her face. "Mama loves you so much. Be good for Uncle Stephen and Aunt Arlene, okay."

"Neal, good boy," he said, grasping for his mother.

"What about, Stephanie?" Grace whispered. "You know how jealous she is of Neal. Do you really think this is such a good idea?"

Arlene touched Grace on the arm to reassure her. "Stephanie will be fine. Now, you two enjoy yourselves."

Stephanie was playing with her dollhouse on the coffee table. She noted that her father was holding Neal in his strong arms. Ignoring the goodbye festivity, she continued to play house.

As soon as the door closed, Neal started to cry. "Oh, Neal," Arlene said, reaching for him. "Don't cry, sweetheart. Mommy and Daddy will be right back."

Neal did not seem to understand, and wailed louder.
"Bounce him around," Stephen said urgently. "Here, let me take him."

No matter how they bounced Neal, he continued to cry.

Stephanie's patience was wearing thin. She placed her hands over her ears. "Make him stop! He's hurting my ears!"
Neal was visibly upset. His nose grew stuffy, his face was red; he drooled uncontrollably and rubbed his eyes with his fist. Soon Madge came down stairs. "What on earth is going on?"

"Neal is upset because his parents are gone," Arlene called over the bellowing.

Madge reached for Neal. "Give me that child." She talked to Neal in soft tones, and he listened. Slowly, she walked out to the kitchen. "Let's get a nice cool snack. It's hot outside, huh, little man?"

As Neal sniffled and grew quiet, the two inexperienced parents sighed and fell upon the sofa. Stephen reached out to caress his daughter; she jerked harshly from his embrace. Not understanding his daughter's plight he shrugged his shoulders and looked at his wife.

That night, Stephanie lay restlessly in bed. She called to Madge as she walked past her door. "Madge! I want a drink of water."

Madge peered inside Stephanie's bedroom. "You've had enough water to float the Titanic, sweet pea."

Stephanie's Emerald Fever

"But, I'm thirsty," she insisted, sleepily wiping a curl from her face.

Suddenly, Madge unlocked the mystery. "Stephanie, did you see your Dad take Neal downstairs to the kitchen?" she asked.

"Yes." Stephanie folded her arms and pushed out her bottom lip. "That's my Daddy, not Neal's Daddy!"

"Don't be selfish, honey. Share your Daddy with Neal. His parents aren't here and Neal is just a little nervous, sugar."

Forcefully, Stephanie kicked the covers backwards with her feet. "I don't want Neal in *my* house!"

Madge was gathering up the covers, but the shock of Stephanie's statement made her stop. "Stephanie! That isn't very nice."

"I don't want Neal in *my house!*" she repeated, kicking the bed with her feet. Grabbing her stuffed unicorn, she violently hurled it out of bed.

Madge tried to quiet her. "Stephanie, don't!"

Stephanie stood up in bed. "Daddy!" she cried louder, "Daddy! Daddy!"

Stephanie's father rushed upstairs, carrying Neal. "What's wrong, short cake?"

Stephanie pointed to Neal. "Him. I want him to go home now!"

Stephen called to Arlene. "Honey, can you come here a minute." When Arlene arrived, he released Neal into her arms. "Could you take care of Neal for a moment?"

"Sure," Arlene agreed, cooing to Neal.

Stephen tried to sooth Stephanie's tantrum. He knelt beside her bed and placed her unicorn under the covers beside her. "Tomorrow, you and Neal can play games outside. You've always wanted someone to play hide and seek with, right?"

Stephanie nodded. "But Neal is too little. His legs are fat and wobbly. He falls down a lot."

Stephen stroked his daughter's head. "That's okay, Steffy. You'll have fun just the same, okay?"

"I guess so," Stephanie yawned.

While Madge watched, Stephen pulled the covers around his daughter. "Now, go to sleep, sweetheart."

Stephanie did not sleep well that night. All night, she visualized Neal in her father's arms and a dreadful jealousy arose inside her. She didn't care if her mother snuggled Neal, but her Dad was *her* Dad, and she wouldn't share him with anyone. Finally, Stephanie drifted off into a deep sleep. A tear,

Stephanie's Emerald Fever

filled with the heaviness of envy, ran down the side of her sleeping face.

That Saturday morning Stephanie seemed calmer. She bounced down the stairs then patiently waited for Neal. "Come on Neal," Stephanie squealed playfully. "I'll race you to the sandbox."

Seeing that Neal was having a difficult time with the stairs, Stephanie went back and helped him down, one step at a time.

Madge was carrying a basket of laundry from the washroom. "Glad to see those two getting along."

"It's like a miracle!" Arlene added, munching on a cluster of grapes. She swept her hair behind her ear. "Wonder what got into her?"

As the two children rushed by, Stephanie's father patted her head, "Atta girl. "I knew you'd come around."

Stephanie smirked; Madge noted something strange about her sudden 'meek' behavior. Nevertheless, she dismissed her suspicion and continued upstairs to put away the wash.

With a glint in her eyes, Arlene popped a grape into her husband's mouth. "Stephen, have you started putting together that grill?"

Annoyed, Stephen scoffed, "Sweetie—Sweetie, I will. I'll do it this evening, okay? It's too hot outside right now. Let me watch the football classics then I promise I'll put the grill together, please."

"Stephen, sweetheart." Arlene's shoulders dropped. "It's a darn DVD. You've watched it many times."

"Please-please," he begged, kissing his wife on the forehead.

Madge walked back down stairs holding the empty clothes basket. "Arlene, eventually you will learn."

Although Arlene looked at Madge with a simple expression, she gave her her full attention. "Tell me Madge, I'm totally stumped." She wiped her damp hands on her jeans.

Madge leaned toward Arlene and whispered, "You can take your man shopping, but you can't take football from your man."

"Amen," Arlene admitted, leaning against the banister. Looking around the room, Madge asked, "Where are the kids?"

"Oh, they're outside playing," Arlene replied.

"In this heat?" Madge asked, holding her cheek.

"Oh you, they're in the shade." She pointed toward the patio. "See, the sandbox is shaded."

Madge shook her finger. "Make sure they get a cool snack in a few, okay."

"Sure, I'll handle it, Madge." She placed her hands on her hips. "I think it's nice that Stephanie is finally coming around," she said, walking toward the patio.

Madge shook her head. "I don't know, Arlene. Something is not right about Stephanie's complete turn-around. Don't forget, I know that young lady very well. When she's nice, you'd better watch out."

Arlene appeared worried. "You think so, Madge?"

"Humph. Hear what I'm saying, honey. I know that daughter of yours." Arlene watched the two playing in the sand. Stephanie was as cute as she could be, and Neal, although he was not her own, was quite an adorable child. "Stephen," she yelled absently. "Can you see the children from there?"

Stephen waved his hand from the sofa and called, "Sure Arlene, I can see the kids through the patio glass. Go ahead and work on your proposal."

Stephanie poured sand into Neal's truck. He held out his hand to feel the sand as it sifted gently into the truck's bed.

While Arlene watched, pleasant thoughts of birthing a son plagued her head, surprisingly she caressed her stomach.

Gradually, Arlene noticed something odd about Stephanie's demeanor. While she studied the children, Stephanie poured the sand. Strangely, Stephanie stared deep into her mother's blue eyes as the sand fell through the sifter. It was one on the coldest stares Arlene had ever seen on her daughter's angelic face; a shudder ran over her body.

Arlene whispered to herself. *"She almost looks evil."* She shook her head. *How could I think such a thing? She's my child.* She dismissed the unimaginable thought then went to finish her work in the study

After an hour, Madge came downstairs. "Has anyone checked on the kids?" She looked toward the patio.

Stephen raised his head from the sofa. "I checked on them during the commercial. Stephanie said they were playing hide and seek."

"Hide and seek, huh? You would think those two would be hungry by now," she said, observing only Stephanie through the glass.

From the sofa Stephen called, "Arlene gave them a snack." Stephen was obviously distracted by the game. "Oh man!" he yelped! "Is he blind or what?"

Madge opened the patio door and stepped outside. The wind blew gently against her dress. "Hi Steffy. Where's your friend, Neal?"

Stephanie continued to play in the sand and obviously ignored Madge. "Steffy. Where is Neal, Honey?"

Stephanie would not look up at Madge. She continued to pour sand out of her bucket and into Neal's dump truck. Still, she didn't answer.

Madge walked up to the sandbox and knelt. She caught Stephanie by the shoulders and forced her to look into her eyes. "Stephanie Denise Andrews! I asked you a question, now you answer me, right now!"

Stephanie started to whine. "Don't, Madge. We were playing hide and seek."

"Yes, and?" Madge asked, not breaking her contact with Stephanie's eyes.

Although, Stephanie played in the sand, she continued to talk. "And Neal hid, but I got tired of playing, so I didn't go seek."

Aggravated, Madge asked, "What do you mean—you didn't go seek?"

Stephanie shrugged. "I didn't go seek him."

Calming her voice Madge questioned, "How long has Neal been hiding, honey?"

Stephanie shrugged, and started to pour sand. "I don't know."

"Sweetie, you need to tell me where Neal is hiding," Madge insisted.

"I don't know, Madge. Don't you like Neal's dump truck? He said I could have it."

Doubting Stephanie's statement, Madge stood up and visibly searched the backyard. "Neal said you could have his truck, huh?"
Stephanie nodded. "He told me before he went to hide and seek."

Agitated, Madge ran toward the house. "Arlene! Stephen!" she called. "Come quick!" Madge tore open the patio door, and explained. "Neal is gone! Stephanie said she doesn't know where he is." Madge checked behind her. "The back yard is gated, he couldn't have gone this way. Help me find him, quick!"

Arlene and Stephen ran from the house. They searched the grounds then they checked the entire house. Searching frantically, they turned over baskets and pillows. They searched the basement and the closets in the bath rooms and bedrooms.

As they searched, they urgently called to Neal. Gradually, the search covered the front yard and the edge of the street.

Stephanie's Emerald Fever

While the three searched hysterically, Stephanie sat calmly in the sand playing with Neal's truck. She smiled to herself. "Neal went home," she whispered lightly.

Madge rushed upstairs to get her purse. "I'm going to drive around the neighborhood. Let's see," she pondered. "What was Neal wearing? I'm so nervous, I can't remember."

"Blue jumpers!" Arlene screamed. "He was wearing blue jumpers and a light blue shirt!"

Stephanie stopped playing, and watched the adults as they scrambled about. "Madge," she said. "I want some juice."

Madge was swinging her keys and purse as she dashed past Stephanie. "Sweetie, you just finished a pouch of juice. I'll get you more juice when I get back."

Stephanie ran up to Madge and pulled on her dress. "But, I'm thirsty now. I want more juice now, I'm thirsty," she whined.

Madge pulled her dress from Stephanie's grasp and stooped down. "Honey," She gazed at Stephanie. "I've got to go! Neal could be in danger."

"But, I want some juice now!" Stephanie started to cry.

Stephen called from the side of the house. "Arlene she's getting on my nerves with that whining. Give her what she wants, now."

Madge huffed as she rushed toward her car. "That's the problem now. Stephanie gets exactly what Stephanie wants and when she wants it."

"Madge, please!" Arlene pleaded. "Not, now."

Stoned faced, Madge turned from Arlene. She was so nervous she could hardly open the car with the remote. Finally, Madge opened the door and the heat rushed out to meet her. "It's hot as an oven in here!" The leather seats were hot to the touch. As Madge was tossing her purse into the front seat she noticed a backpack filled with clothes. "What this?" Picking up Neal's overstuffed bag, Madge got out the car. "Why, these are Neal's things." Her voice became cracked as her breathing quickened. "Dear God, why would anyone put Neal's things in *my* car?"

Madge looked in the back seat. She didn't see any sign of Neal. "Humph," she sighed nervously. On a whim, she got out of the car and flung open the back door.

Much to her horror, there, on the floorboard, was Neal's lifeless body. Madge's trembling hand flew over her mouth. Being mortified by the sight, she screamed over and over.

Thinking the worst, Stephanie and Arlene ran towards the car.

Madge was clearly shaken. Pointing inside the car, she trembled hysterically.

Stephen trotted up to the car. "What is it, Madge?"

Stephanie's Emerald Fever

"It's, it's—Neal!!" she said, with a loud sob. "It's, it's Neal."

Stephen squatted down to investigate. "My God, Madge! How did Neal get in your car?" He picked up Neal's limp body.

Stephen rubbed his forehead then felt for a pulse. "Lord! He's hot! Arlene! Call 911. Hyperthermia. I can't feel a pulse."

"Is he going to be okay?" Arlene sobbed. She tugged on her husband's arm to stroke the unresponsive child.

"I don't know," Stephen cried, holding the child to his chest. "I just don't know. Let's get him inside."

Stephanie whined. "Daddy, I didn't get a drink."

This time Stephen ignored Stephanie as he marched toward the living room to place the dying child on the sofa. "Madge, get some towels and some water!" he ordered. "We've got to cool him down."

By the time the ambulance arrived, Neal had passed away. The temperature in the car was unbearable; Neal had been in the car, much too long.

Stephanie sat on the sofa and watched, as the three huddled and sobbed. Feeling like it was his fault, Stephen's blood pressure reached stroke level. The paramedics warned him to calm down.

"You don't understand," he yelled, violently pushing them aside. "That's my brother's son! That's my brother's only child!" Stephen buried his face in his hands and sobbed out loud. "The game was more important to me than the kids!"

Madge grabbed Stephen and held him quietly. He laid his head on her shoulder and wept. "Madge, I killed my brother's child!" he whimpered.

"Sh-sh, Stephen," she said. Madge raised his contorted face and looked into his swollen eyes. "Sweetie, God was ready for Neal. And, nothing could have stopped that request."

Arlene and Madge managed to call Grace and Allen. The bad news was more than Grace could take; she was put to bed, immediately.

When things calmed down a bit, Madge decided to question a cheerful little Stephanie. She had her doubts about what actually happened to Neal. Madge took Stephanie by the hand and led her upstairs. Once they were in her bedroom she placed Stephanie on her bed.

"Stephanie. Do you know why we're here?"

Stephanie smiled. "I like your room. Everything is so big."

Ignoring Stephanie's statement Madge continued. She knew that little trick, all too well. "Stephanie. I know Neal didn't put his things in my car. And you'd better tell me the truth. I'm not your mother and I'm not your father, you know what that means, right?"

Playing with the pocket on Madge's dress, Stephanie said, "I don't know what happened to Neal. He said he wanted to go home," she stated innocently.

Lifting her chin, Madge looked sternly into Stephanie's eyes. "And...what—did—you—do!"

Stephanie stuck her fingers in her mouth, making barely audible sounds.

"Take your fingers out of your mouth and tell me what happened," she scolded.

Stephanie took her fingers out of her mouth then wrung the bottom of her blouse. "I told Neal...you would...take him home...today. So, I put him in the car...and told him...to wait."

Madge grimaced. "Stephanie. My car was locked. How did Neal get inside?"

Stephanie shrugged, but didn't answer.

"If you think this is a game, young lady, you are sadly mistaken."

Stephanie held her head down. "I got your keys and unlocked the car." She looked up at Madge. "I told Neal to get in."

"My God!" Madge's hand flew over her mouth.

Unknowingly, Stephanie told Madge the entire story. "When I closed the door, he stood up in the back seat and started crying... but I told him to wait for you. Then he turned really red, then he threw up."

Tears stood in Madge's eyes. "Honey, why did you tell your father you were playing hide and go seek?"

"Cause—cause," she stammered. "Cause-Neal stopped crying and I didn't want Daddy to hold him."

Before Madge realized what she was saying, she blurted, "Stephanie, you watched Neal suffer in that hot car? *Jesus*!!" She grabbed Stephanie and held her. "Oh, Sweet Jesus!" With tears streaming down her brown face, Madge held Stephanie in her arms and rocked her.

Awaken by the loud cries of her own voice Stephanie screamed out, "I didn't mean to hurt, Neal!" She buried her face in the scratchy hay and sobbed. "I didn't mean to hurt him, Madge!" She grabbed a handful of hay and closed her fist tightly. "I just wanted my Daddy to myself. I didn't mean..."

This time, Madge was no where around. No one was there to comfort her. It had been many years since she thought about Neal and that awful day. She never took responsibility for Neal's death, but today, she became fully aware of her selfish

Stephanie's Emerald Fever

behavior. Wiping her eyes, she realized she must deal with her present situation.

Stephanie was glad morning had come. Reliving Neal's death had been too emotional for her; she sat numb with the dark memories of his last days. Now, she understood the move to New York. Obviously, her family had worn out their welcome.

As promised, Ma left milk and bread for Stephanie. Despite this small comfort she still had an uneasy feeling that something else was wrong. Pulling straw from her hair, Stephanie sat upright in the hay. Immediately, she crouched and listened. Chickens fluttered about in a frenzy beneath her. Hearing an echoing yelp of barking dogs Stephanie stared at the barn door. A cold chill ran over her as she strained to listen.

Suddenly, the barn door burst open. There, in the smoky mist of the morning, a team of men from the Andrews Plantation stood before her. Sweating horses, abused by harsh riding, snorted smoky vapors from their noses and mouths. At the sight of Stephanie, hound dogs leaped wildly into the air straining at their taut leashes.

Stephanie wanted to cry out but remained still.

"Come on down here!" a man yelled. "We know you is up there."

They pointed their guns and Stephanie did as she was told. She could see three men but wondered if there was also a fourth man present. Timidly, Stephanie held her dress and descended the ladder that lead from the hayloft. Standing before the mercy of the men, she humbled herself by casting her eyes downward.

"I don't know why Old Man Andrews wants you in one piece," said one man. "I guess you worth more alive than you is dead, even ifn you is crazy. Now git on out dare!"

The man shoved Stephanie out of the barn and into the foggy morning light. Wearing M'dere's clunky shoes Stephanie stumbled on an exposed root. She tripped into a nearby pine tree striking her cheekbone hard against the jagged bark. As she was getting up a man gruffly kicked her.

"That's what ya gets fer makin' me git up early." Caught-up in the fabric of M'dere's large dress Stephanie rolled over, tearing the dress away from the waistline. She landed on her back; her hair littered with dirt and grass. Breathing loudly Stephanie held her bruised cheek and searched the sky.

Feeling as though she was being unjustly treated Stephanie tried to plead her case…carefully, of course. "I ain't done nuthin' to you," she muttered. "Ifn' you jest tells me what you wants me to do Sa, I'll do it."

"Oh, she tryin' to be smart huh, Joshua?" said one man.

Joshua stroked his gun and spit. "I think you is right, Luke." He grabbed Stephanie and yanked her from the ground. Supported by Joshua's brute strength, she stood limply before his evil presence. The large bruise on Stephanie's right cheek caused her eye to wince under the intense throbbing pain. Her eye watered and blinked excessively as she squinted at Joshua.

"You lookin' lack you wanna fight Old Joshua. Is that why you is a'lookin' at me? Ya wanna hit Old Joshua?" Shaking Stephanie like she was made of straw, Joshua grabbed her by the collar and pulled her near his face. His foul body odor reminded her of the wild hog. The whiskey on his breath was as strong as the stiff stubble on his square chin. Feeling as though her breath would be cut off, Stephanie raised her hands to her throat.

Joshua squealed, "Ya'll saw that! This she gal wuz a'tryin' to hit me! Why you..." Joshua raised his fist and swung backwards to deliver his best blow. His large fist came down with a swift jerk stopping short of Stephanie's face. He looked at his fist then noticed that his elbow was being held captive by one of the men. "Let 'er go Joshua! What did Old Man Andrews tel' us when we left?"

Joshua looked at his hungry fist then at Stephanie. He tightened his other fist around her neck once more. Pointing to the woods he said, "Normally, we'd drag your black hide back to the plantation but I guess Old Man Andrews wants you to look purty at the sell."

Joshua tossed Stephanie toward Luke and Luke tossed her to the third man. When the third man caught Stephanie in his arms he turned her where she could face him. The man grabbed Stephanie by her cheeks and squeezed until her lips puckered. While looking down on her he said, "Ifn a slave gots whelps on his hide at the sell, the buyer thinks he's either hard headed or a runaway. And, sweet thang," he pinched Stephanie's cheek and slapped her lightly. "He wants all he can git outta you."

After spitting a wad of chewing tobacco on the ground, Luke tied Stephanie's hands with a small piece of rope. Two men picked Stephanie up and placed her awkwardly upon a saddleless horse then they tied the bridle around her rope-bound hands. Joshua secured the barking dogs while Luke walked back toward the barn and slammed the heavy door.

Stephanie didn't recall very much about the trip home. Other than her brutal experiences with the Andrews' men, and the memory of Neal's death, she was sadder than she'd ever been.

Chapter Twelve

Is There Freedom in Shrimp Gumbo?

"I would faint, too, if I had to wear that much fabric all day long."

Chapter Twelve

Stephanie had been locked away in a wooden box that resembled an outhouse. All morning she peered through a small hole in the wooden door. All appeared calm when suddenly, she saw a large black woman walking across the yard toward her substandard prison. With steps that were both heavy and quick, the woman's no nonsense demeanor around her like a thick fog. By her uniform Stephanie could tell she was a housemaid. This housemaid didn't work in the kitchen and she didn't take care of children, her job was to wash clothes and simply take care of the large mansion.

As the woman moved closer Stephanie studied the form of her muscular arms. The tightness of her short sleeves strapped her muscles. Her dark skin glistened with oil in the midday heat. A nose that flared like a snorting bull and small deep-set eyes told Stephanie she was ill-tempered in nature and perhaps a force to be reckoned with. The woman's tightly drawn lips meant her life was a private affair and not for public discussion.

Peering inside the humid box, the woman sneered at Stephanie. "Looka here, gal, Massa done tol' me to clean you up fer da sell." Leaning her weight against the door, she removed the large iron latch. "Don't you try nuttin'. Ifn you do, I'm liable to break yore neck," she warned, pulling the door open. "Ifn you try to run, I ain't gonna chase ya. One of dem mens is gonna put a hole in ya. Ya hear me, gal!" Stephanie nodded. The woman looked Stephanie up and down. "I gotta wash you up then wash dat stuff on yore haid." Gruffly, the woman snatched straw from Stephanie's head. "You shore is filthy."

"Massa plans to git plenty fer ya." She grabbed Stephanie by the wrist and snatched her from the box. Pulling her by the arm the woman led Stephanie to a room on the back porch. When the woman opened the door of the room, Stephanie saw a small bed made from unfinished wood. She also saw what was called a number three tub, a chamber bucket, and a change of clothing.

Shoving Stephanie inside the room the woman unsympathetically informed her, "You is one lucky gal. Mister Jones is gonna buy you straight out." She lifted Stephanie's face in her large hands to survey her bruises. "All you gots is jest dat one black eye and dat dere scrape on yore forehead? Humph! You is a lucky chile to be ah run-away. Hadda been me, dayda beat me to death."

The woman hastily removed Stephanie's soiled clothing and hurled her, gasping for breath, into the large tub which was filled with hot soapy water. With a soft brush, she started to scrub Stephanie like a hog being prepared for the county fair. Stephanie would have enjoyed a bath; however her delicate skin had several painful cuts and abrasions so she did have objections to this harsh treatment. Sadly, her frail complaints were drowned out by soap bubbles and the constant splashing of water.

Like a dutiful slave, the woman washed Stephanie's hair, rinsing it with buckets of clear water. While briskly rubbing Stephanie's head with a towel the woman explained, "Mister Jones is gonna be here fer suppa tonight then he gonna take a good look-at-cha in da mornin'."

After Stephanie had her bath and shampoo, the woman rubbed oil on her dry skin. Using the same oil, she greased then plaited Stephanie's hair. M'dere's methods of combing hair were angelic in comparison to this woman's torture. Stephanie's head was snatched and pulled. Her hair was torn out and tossed aside with little regard to the pain it might be causing her.

After the woman finished combing the snarls out of Stephanie's hair, she parted it into small sections then plaited the damp hair. Rolling each plait downward she tucked the ends underneath the base of the plait. When the woman completed Stephanie's hair, she had eight plaits on her head. The tucking process had hidden the ends of the plaits which made each plait an isolated knot on Stephanie's head. For a finishing touch, the woman wrapped a red kerchief around her damp head then tucked a knot in the very front of her head.

Stephanie tried to coax the woman into a conversation but all she said was, "Humph!"

Stephanie was dressed in a long, red and white checkered dress with a large white collar and an apron. She was given thick cotton hose and masculine looking shoes that surprisingly, almost fit. When the woman was finished with Stephanie she looked her up and down. "Yous look da part," admitted the woman. "Now, ya gotta acts da part. Forgit dat stuff you learnt in da field."

Stephanie smiled wryly. "Oh, I will." Hearing music again, Stephanie's trained ear followed every note of the lively melody. The window in the little room had a view through the kitchen. With the door opened to the formal dining area, Stephanie was able to see a girl about her age playing the piano. 'So that's our little Mozart,' she thought.

Stephanie had never seen the girl before. She was fair-skinned and very beautiful. Golden ringlets hung down her back and ornamented tucking combs of white and pink roses supported her hair just above the temples. Her dress was pink and white taffeta. Stephanie could not help but stare. "Who is she?" she asked the woman, "Is she an Andrews too?"

The woman was rude but answered. "Dat is Old Man Andrews' pride 'n joy. Dat be his granddaughter, Cassandra. She is always been here. Her mother died when she was birthed."

"She's beautiful," Stephanie observed rubbing her own scarf clad head.

"Yas, Sah, she is beauty-full inside 'n out. And one day she will marry some rich man 'n move clean away from here," she said harshly.

Cassandra stopped practicing. "Mother Andrews, I'm finished," she called softly. "May I go now?"

Stephanie strained to see into the formal dining area. "Where is she going?"

Mopping water from the floor, the woman crowed. "Now, dat ain't none of yore business. Ifn you must know, she is sickly. The doctor will be here fer 'er soon."

"What's wrong with her?" Stephanie asked, straining to get another look.

The woman stopped mopping and stood still. With her hand on her hip, she held the mop and gawked at Stephanie. Suddenly, she started mopping again. "Why, you 'bout a nosey critter," she sassed. "I don't know. She jest have faintin' spells sometimes."

"I would faint too if I had to wear that much fabric all day."

Stephanie's Emerald Fever

The large woman squeezed the water out of the mop. "Hush up! It ain't da dress. She don't start ailin' 'til we's 'bout to finish suppa. She go to git up then she faints dead away."

Bell had placed a plate of cold beans, cornbread, and a tall glass of buttermilk in the window of the little room. The woman handed Stephanie the plate and the buttermilk. Sitting down on the floor, Stephanie examined the food. It was almost second nature to now use her fingers when eating. Hungrily, Stephanie scooped up fingers full of juicy nourishment. With her mouth crammed full, Stephanie added, "Sounds like Cassandra is eating something that's, like, making her sick," she muffed through her chewing.

The woman folded her large arms and stared down on Stephanie. "Are ya tryin' to 'cuse Mama Bell of poisonin' Old Man Andrews' granddaughter?"

Stephanie continued to chew. "No, I'm just saying that if she is fainting after she, like, eats," she swallowed hard. "She must be eating something that's, like, making her sick. Think about it. What is she eating when she gets sick?"

Stephanie reached for the buttermilk and took a thirsty gulp. Her cheeks puckered immediately. Holding the rancid milk in her puckered mouth, her eyes widened with surprise. With her face twisted into a nasty frown. Stephanie swallowed grudgingly. "What the heck is this mess?" She wiped her mouth with the back of her hand leaving a trail of buttermilk on her cheek. "Eeewww! That milk is spoiled!" she said, pushing the glass aside.

"Well, ifn you ain't gonna drink it, I knows plenty of folks who will!"

Stephanie pinched her nose. "Ew-Ew-Ew! They can have it!"

"Humph! You don't know what good is. Gimmie dat!"

After recovering from the unpleasant experience, Stephanie scooped up more food with her fingers. "Can you remember what Cassandra is eating when she faints?"

Walking and pondering the woman thought for a moment. "Well, it don't happen ery day, only on da days we is havin' shrimp gumbo."

Stephanie stood up, bean juice dripping down her chin. "That's it!" she exclaimed. "She's allergic to shellfish!"

"Urgic what?" The woman repeated with a baffled frown.

"Just don't give her any tonight and see what happens."

"Nope! Not me," she shook her large head. "Bell ain't gonna beat me wit no kitchen spoon. That yalla woman is ticky 'bout her food. Why you worryin' 'bout this anyways? You is gonna be sold on tomorrow mornin'." The woman started to make the bed.

Stephanie's Emerald Fever

Stephanie sat back down on the floor with her legs sprawled to her side. "The reason I'm concerned is that I am highly allergic to shellfish." She violently grabbed her throat. "If I, like, eat it, my throat closes up and I can't breathe." Her eyes bulged. "I could even die from eating it!"

Stephanie searched the woman's eyes for compassion; instead utter horror contorted her face. "Glory be! Dat *is* scary!"

"It's worth a try," Stephanie pleaded. "Spill it—drop it—put a fly in it, but don't let her eat it again."

The woman lit a kerosene lamp and turned it down low. She walked over to the bed pulled back the covers and exposed rough textured sheets. "Now, how umma 'splain dis to dem, witout lookin' plum crazy, lack you? Half da time I ain't even allowed in da kitchen," she sassed.

"I don't know," Stephanie admitted. Just think of something. My father was allergic to shellfish and so was his grandfather. It stands to reason that—that—"

The woman seemed puzzled but interested. "Yas? Go on, gal. This is soundin' like 'fessional stuff."

"Nothing." Stephanie cast her eyes to the floor. In a muted tone she whispered. "Just do it."

"Humph! I'll see what I can do 'bout dat." After gathering Stephanie's dress and the damp towels, the woman placed her hand on the leather strap to open the door. She stopped abruptly. "Nigh thinkin' back on it." She placed her brown finger to her temple. "The nigh dat chile's mama went into labor 'n died, she had et ah big bowl of Bell's gumbo." She turned toward Stephanie. "They took dat yungn' 'n she was powerful sick, too! They thought she was gonna die jest lacka mama."

The entire idea made the woman's heart race. "Bell had jest been bought at this here plantation. She ah started cookin' dat old Frenchie stuff." As if on fire, the woman suddenly rushed out the door.

Stephanie looked through the little window and patiently awaited her fate, Cassandra made herself beautiful while she awaited hers. At six o'clock, Cassandra was dressed magnificently for dinner. She floated gracefully down the alabaster staircase. The elegant table was set with a lovely spread of tasty foods.

From her dank room on the back porch, Stephanie could smell fried chicken and buttery mashed potatoes. The smell of fresh corn on the cob made her mouth water. She imagined what the table must look like with cloth napkins, fine china, and elegant silver.

Although she was locked away, light conversation drifted to her clammy little room. At home, she was the center of attention during dinner. Now, dreadful wooden boards separated her from the enjoyment of the formal dining area.

Stephanie's Emerald Fever

When the guest arrived, the living room became alive with laughter and merriment. "Mister Jones," Stephanie heard Andrews say. "I've got one prime gal for you to see — in the morning, of course."

"Of course," a deep southern male voice replied. "I was told she's strong and a hard worker."

Old Man Andrews coughed. "Why, yes. Yes, she is, Sah. Cooks almost as good as my Bell. You know I only sell my best to friends and associates. Don't let her fool you. She'll try to make you think she can't cook a thang. But that ain't nothing you can't rectify, Mister Jones. I assure you will be happy with this gal."

After overhearing Old Man Andrews' conversation with Mr. Jones, Stephanie realized she was about to play a major role in a scam. Old Man Andrews didn't consider her prime stock, he regarded her as damaged goods. And the worst part was that he planned to pawn her off on this unsuspecting soul.

Stephanie heard the soft familiar voice of Mrs. Andrews. "Oh, you men folk are always talkin' business over dinner. Tell me Mister Jones, how is yore lovely wife? Has she recovered from her operation?"

"Well, that's why I'm here. We need more help around the place with her ailing and all. I'm just glad that my old friend here has just the gal I need."

After hearing the conversation between Old Man Andrews and Mister Jones, Stephanie sat down on the side of the bed, she folded her arms and sulked. "Humph! Andrews will need a lawyer if he tries to sell me to that guy!" Sliding between the cool covers, Stephanie realized she had not slept in a bed for quite some time. House slaves did sleep in real beds but first she would need to learn how to cook. Her culinary experiences were limited to precooked food specially prepared for the microwave.

Stephanie heard a bell ring. She turned her face toward the window and listened. Mrs. Andrews called, "Bell, bring the gumbo." She addressed Mister Jones, "Bell makes the best gumbo in this area. It's become a family favorite. We try to eat it at least three times a month. It's difficult to find all the ingredients," she informed proudly. "But we manage."

That was Stephanie's cue. She leaped from her bed, stood up, and tried to peek inside the kitchen. She saw the woman who had dressed her. Beating on the wall she tried desperately to get her attention. The woman never heard her. Picking up the servings of gumbo, Bell proceeded toward the dining area.

Knowing that one bite of shrimp could possibly kill Cassandra, Stephanie paced. She reasoned that she must have been sipping the broth when she became ill or fainted.

"Gumbo! Oh, how wonderful!" she heard Cassandra exclaim. "Last time I didn't quite get the chance to enjoy it before I became ill. Somehow, I never get to enjoy it."

Stephanie's Emerald Fever

Stephanie had to think fast. She beat on the wall louder and louder and even called out a few times. The only person who heard her cries was Mama Bell and she closed the window to shut out Stephanie's excessive noise.

Mimicking M'dere's gestures, Stephanie got down on her knees, pressed her hands together and made a steeple. "Lord, I know you don't, like, hear from me much. And from the looks of things you must be pretty ticked at me right about now. Well, I don't blame you; I've made a mess of things. This time I'm not asking for a pony, like I did when I was seven. I'm not asking anything for myself. I'm asking that you not let Cassandra have that gumbo. Please! Then I want to go home. I had to throw that part in because I really-really do want to go home. I've been through a lot these last few days. Please, like, show us some mercy, Amen. Oh, and thanks for sending Zeb to look for me."

Stephanie finished her prayer just as Bell spilled Cassandra's bowl of gumbo into the tray.

"Oops! I'm sorry," Bell admitted. "Let me git you anotha bowl, Sher."

'Another bowl,' Stephanie thought. 'They're going to kill that poor child, after all.'

Mister Jones patted his belly and prepared to eat his gumbo. "You know, Andrews. Since my wife has been sick, I've been reading a lot of medical books." He blew on his spicy gumbo.

"I read one article that said some people are actually allergic to shrimp and other shellfish."

Andrews replied, "Shore 'nuff, Mister Jones? Well, I haven't ever heard of such a thing."

"Oh yes, it is a fact, Mr. Andrews. It causes one's throat to constrict until they feel like someone is choking the life out of them. Some people even pass out from the lack of oxygen — from what I can understand," he added.

Mrs. Andrews giggled. "What a fascinatin' find, Mister Jones. I'm glad that you shared that interestin' fact with us. I'm relieved that we are not allergic to this, ah, shell animal."

"Granddaddy," Cassandra spoke softly. "I hate to interrupt grown folks when they is talkin', but I have somethin' to say." She clasped one hand over the other and waited to speak.

Proud of his parenting skills, Andrews encouraged, "Go right ahead, child."

Cassandra continued. "Well, when one of my faintin' spells overtakes me, I feel that same way," She leaned forward. "Like somebody is chokin' me, I mean." The stare in her blue eyes was sincere.

Mrs. Andrews looked at her husband and then at Mister Jones. She chuckled lightly. "Why, that's just nonsense, Shugah. We all know that you've got a bad heart. The doctor said so." She glared at Mister Jones. "Mister Jones is hardly a physician just because he read a book, dear. Now, Bell will bring you another bowl shortly."

Wide-eyed and scared, Cassandra begged, "I don't mean to be impolite, but I don't wanna eat it, Mother Andrews."

Awkwardly looking around the room, Mrs. Andrews grinned sheepishly. "Why Shugah, nobody is going to foce you ta eat it."

Old Man Andrews sputtered. "Quite all right. You don't have to eat it, dear. Jones, you might be onto something. I might need to read that medical book of yours."

When Bell brought another bowl of gumbo, Cassandra refused it. That night, she walked away from the table instead of being carried to her room.

From the dank room on the back porch, Stephanie felt a victory had been won in favor of Cassandra. During the night, Stephanie prepared for her fate. Whatever the consequences were, she would humbly accept them.

Chapter Thirteen

I've Been in Your Skin

"My name is Stephanie!"

Chapter Thirteen

Stephanie tried hard to stay awake. She heard every noise known to man and some noises that were not. Her mind conjured up demons and warlocks. She could swear someone was lurking in the kitchen just above her head.

Stephanie crept toward the boarded-up window that led to the kitchen. She peered through the cracks in the unfinished boards. A glowing light moved hauntingly about the kitchen. Stephanie pressed her eye closer; she could tell the person in the kitchen had a small frame. Because the individual was dressed in white from head to toe, it was difficult to tell who it was.

Stephanie found a larger hole and pressed her eye against the board. "It's Cassandra." Immediately, Stephanie wondered if she could make Cassandra hear her. She made a noise. "Psst, Psst."

Cassandra turned on her heels, almost dropping the lamp. "Who's dare?" Stephanie continued to make the noise; Cassandra followed the queer sound. When she discovered the noise came from the room outside the kitchen, she placed the lamp on the table. Carefully, she walked over to the tightly bolted window, her sleeping bonnet shading her eyes. "Who's dare? Is somebody in dat room outdare?"

In response, Stephanie pecked gently on the wood.

Cassandra pulled the giant latch off the window and opened the wooden shutters. "You'd betta go to sleep in dare. I ain't playin' with you none."

Stephanie giggled. Cassandra's English was horrible and nothing like the dinner conversation she'd heard earlier.

"You'd betta stop that cacklin'. You gonna wake my folks."

Stephanie giggled again, this time more loudly. She covered her mouth to muffle her laughter. Suddenly, Cassandra opened the window, exposing Stephanie. "Well, if it ain't Miss Funny Bones."

Stephanie snickered. *'Where'd she get that one?'* In Stephanie's opinion, Cassandra's English was like the kids from a Huck Finn movie. She found it hilarious.

"What's so dang funny, darkie?"

Stephanie flinched, she was terribly insulted. "Who are you calling 'darkie'?" What Cassandra heard was a series of grunts and squeals.

Stephanie's Emerald Fever

Cassandra picked up the kerosene lamp. She held it up to get a better look at Stephanie. "My-my. I do think you is a girl darkie." She leaned closer. "It's hard to tell the boys from the gals." She sniffed. "They all smells alike, and they all looks alike. But, I think you is a girl. I kin tell by that rag tied 'round your haid." Cassandra walked closer. "Let me git a closer look at you. Now I ain't sked, so don't you start nuttin, ya hear?"

Standing in the darkness, Stephanie showed white eyes and teeth. She stifled a smile as the girl came closer to the window.

Shining the light on Stephanie, Cassandra smiled back. "Well, well, well, just look at you." She fluttered her eyes. "I bet you ain't never seen nuttin as pretty as me before."

Stephanie shook her head to agree. "You purty," she said slowly. Stephanie was confused. For the life of her she could not understand why her English was so poor. Each time she tried to talk to someone her own race, they couldn't understand a word she was saying.

Then it dawned on her, she could speak some English, but she didn't know how much. Now was a good time to find out. "Ome er," she grunted. "Ome er," she repeated, beckoning Cassandra with her hand.

Cassandra asked, "What ya'll want? Don't try nuttin, now." Cassandra retrieved a large wooden spoon from the cabinet. "I kin make a powerful sting with dis here spoon." As if to threaten Stephanie, she lunged at her.

Stephanie jumped back. "Why you!" This game was not funny anymore and she didn't like being treated like a caged animal. Reaching her dark hand through a slot in the window, she beckoned Cassandra once again.

"If I come over dare, you betta not try to hurt me."

Stephanie shook her head. "No hurt," she said, coarsely.

"You'd betta not. They'll hang you fore mornin' ifn you do."

That did it! Stephanie could not imagine why people wanted to hurt her. She hadn't done anything particularly rash.

Deciding she no longer wanted to be friends with Cassandra, Stephanie walked away from the window and into the darkness. Once in the darkness, she folded her arms and sat on the bed.

Although Stephanie was poor and didn't own a thing, she still owned her pride. Whether her pride was Andrews' or human, she was not going to endure this kind of humiliation for anyone.

Cassandra was surprised. "Well I declare, I could almost swear you was ashunnin' me. You git back over here this instant."

Stephanie shook her head emphatically. *No!*

"Well, it's not like you have feelings or anything. You acting like you done had your feelin' hurt."

Stephanie nodded her head. *Yes!*

"But, you ain't got no feelings," Cassandra insisted. "Not like us Christian bone Americans."

Stephanie's heart sank. Those were the cruelest words ever invented by man. As her emotions grew obvious, Stephanie hid a sniffle.

Cassandra continued to state her case. "I know, you ain't got no feelins 'cause my Granddaddy done tol me you ain't got none."

Stephanie was wounded. 'How dare her insinuate she had no feelings just because her skin was black.' She closed her lips tightly, but a weak whimper escaped. In the darkness, she turned her back toward Cassandra.

Astonished, Cassandra added, "Well, I'll be. Granddaddy was wrong. I do believe I hurt this gal's feelins."

Stephanie nodded. *Yes!*

"Humph!" she said. "Well, well, well." Cassandra moved back to the table with the lamp. Placing the lamp on the table she said, "I jest came down here to git me some of Bell's tea cakes. I didn't eat much before I retired for bed."

Cassandra pulled a large crock toward her. The top clattered loudly as she removed it. Tilting the jar, she removed a tea cake and placed it in her mouth. "You want one of these, gal?" she muffed.

Although, Stephanie was angry, she wasn't stupid. She nodded for Cassandra to give her a tea cake.

Cassandra swallowed. "I bet you ain't never had nuttin' like this, have you, darkie?" She handed the tea cake to Stephanie. Stephanie accepted the tea cake then walked toward the back of the room to eat it. After all, stale or not, Bell's tea cakes were still delicious.

Cassandra picked up her gown and went toward the table to get the lamp. "I betta be going now, darkie. The doctor's comin' to see me first thing in the mornin'," she said with a sigh.

Stephanie moved toward the window. She wanted so badly to communicate with Cassandra. "Wait!" she called.

Alarmed Cassandra turned. "Did you say somethin'? Who else in dare wit you, gal?" Cassandra brought the lamp back to the window. She held the light high and peered inside the small space. "I know I heard somebody say somethin'."

Stephanie's Emerald Fever

Stephanie placed her hand over her full lips, she did say something. "Ah said...I said..." She listened to herself. "I said wait," she finished proudly.

"Why listen to you," Cassandra grinned. "You kin talk. Granddaddy said ya'll was tricky."

Stephanie spoke clear and loud. "No, I'm not tricky, Cassandra."

"Well did you ever! And *it* knows my name."

Stephanie frowned. "Cassandra, I'm not an *it*."

Cassandra placed her hand to her breast. "And *it's* trying to be funny, but she ain't."

Infuriated, Stephanie blasted. "Would you just listen!"

"No Mam. I ain't gonna listen to nuttin a gal darkie has to say," she sassed.

Throwing her hands in the air, Stephanie pleaded. "Stop that! It's time you realized we're all human!" Angrily, she paced the floor. "I don't belong in this cage anymore than you do. Especially, to be sold!"

"I'm gonna git Granddad! I done found something he might wanna see; a proper talking darkie!"

Stepping toward Cassandra Stephanie pleaded. "Cassandra don't! He'd never understand." She shook her head. "Heck, I don't even understand."

Suspiciously, Cassandra questioned, "Is you one of them witch doctors?"

"A what? Witch! Really. Really. Are you, like, kidding?" Crushed, Stephanie tossed her kerchief to the floor. "Where do you people get these ideas?"

"Kin you prove you ain't no witch doctor. You knows my name."

Walking over to the window, Stephanie explained. "That's because I asked a woman who you were! I heard you playing Beethoven, so I thought you were more intelligent than that!"

Shocked, Cassandra sneered. "Beethoven, only a itch would know that!" she sassed.

"Oh, forget it," Stephanie screamed, pacing the floor.

Cassandra blinked modestly. "You liked my piano playing?"

"Yes. I did. But, that was before I found out you're just like the rest of them. I thought you were special."

"Special?" Cassandra swallowed.

Stephanie's Emerald Fever

"Yes, special," Stephanie mocked.

Casting her eyes toward the floor, Cassandra admitted, "I'm sorry, but I haven't been taught how to talk to darkies."

Turning on her heels with finger extended Stephanie discharged. "That's another thing. My name is Ste-phan-ie. That's Stephanie! Can you say Stephanie? Not darkie! Not Gal! But, Stephanie! No one is named darkie! What kind of race is a darkie! That's, like, totally degrading!"

Cassandra was stunned. "But I—"

"And another thing," Stephanie stormed. "How would you like it if I called you Whitie?" she prissed. "How would you like being in here, instead of me?" Walking over to the window, Stephanie admitted, "Sweetie, I've been in your shoes and I've learned a lot. Do you want to trade lives with me?"

Cassandra was speechless. "I...I...I ain't never been told off by no dark—I mean a Dark Brown person before. I don't know if I should have you whipped, shot, or hung."

"Why not do all three!" Disappointed, Stephanie walked away from the window. "Just, go away," she shunned. "Close the darn window and go away! I'm tired, okay. Good night, Missy Cassandra," she said sarcastically.

Cassandra reared up. "Looka here, you can't tell me to go away in my own home."

"Really!" Stephanie brayed, her neck straining. "Well, I said, get lost! And, I meant that!"

Stephanie had turned her back, but decided to speak with Cassandra face to face. Shaking her brown finger at Cassandra, she explained, "You need to take that backwoods attitude back upstairs and put it to bed!"

Cassandra grew nervous. "You sure you ain't no witch?"

Stephanie's voice sliced the darkness. "Cassandra, get real! Please!" She walked over to the bed and threw herself upon it. Folding her arms across her breast she announced, "I'm finished. I don't have anything else to say to someone who thinks like you." She mumbled to herself. "And they say 'I' need an attitude adjustment." Ignoring Cassandra, she turned over on her side.

Suddenly, there was an eerie silence. Holding the kerosene lamp, Cassandra stood still. A long sigh pierced the darkness. "You are right. I ain't never thought about it like that before. I'm sorry." With her back turned, Cassandra picked up her gown. "I'm sorry, Step-phan-e." She shamefully walked away.

Finally speaking her mind, Stephanie suppressed her heart rate then fell asleep.

Bright and early the next morning, Stephanie heard the door being unlatched and opened. The big woman stood solemnly before her. Stephanie sat upright in bed to hear her verdict. "Massa Andrews said you is free to go."

Stephanie's eyes brightened. "What? I don't understand. Are you saying free to go back to the quarters or free to go period?"

"You is free to go period! Massa felt bad after Mister Jones save Cassandra. He is beholdin' to Mister Jones now. He decided to sell him anotha gal. Addie. She a real house gal. She new on dis here plantation and she's a tad might better'n you. Plus, Bell done taught 'er to cook."

"*Sweet*! This is awesome news!" Stephanie scooted to the side of the bed and reached for her red kerchief. "May I have my new shoes?"

"Why, shore," the woman beamed.

"And no one will hurt me?" Stephanie hesitated, looking cautiously around the room.

"Not a tall."

"I can go see M'dere now?"

The woman nodded. "Shore. Now scat!"

Stephanie put on her masculine-looking shoes and opened the door to the room. Her feet were still bruised and sore but she wanted to see M'dere and Sam one last time. She didn't know how to start her life as a free person, but she would find out.

Leaving all thoughts of Cassandra behind, Stephanie stepped out of the small room. She inhaled the fresh morning air and stretched. With a large smile stretched across her lips her eyes beheld Old Jacob's beautifully manicured lawn. Looking into the distance she could see the shoddy old track houses.

Stephanie took her first steps toward freedom when she chose the path leading toward the track houses. She walked slowly at first but as she walked, a surge of deliverance electrified her body and she started to run, Sweet Freedom! After getting her breath, she leaped into the air with joy-charged feet.

Hearing someone urgently calling, Stephanie turned in response. Vigorously waving her hands and shouting the woman tried desperately to make Stephanie hear her cries. Stephanie stopped running and strained to listen. "Don't run!" the woman called. "*Oh Lordy Jesus*!! Don't Ru—"

Unexpectedly, Stephanie heard the echo of a shot being fired. Simultaneously, she vividly smelled the burning stench of gun powder. As if in slow motion, Stephanie fell to the ground hearing the woman's terrifying screams.

Stephanie lay still on Old Jacob's beautifully manicured lawn. Her staring gaze admired the splendor of a dew-drenched blade of grass. With lips parted, she gasped for her last…life-sustaining…breath.

Chapter Fourteen

A Long Journey to Nowhere

"What a night!"

Chapter Fourteen

Gasping for a precious breath of air, Stephanie woke up. Madge was sitting beside, her pressing a wet towel against her forehead. Dazed, she gazed groggily around the room. She was in her own bedroom, with her own furnishings. This was her bed and not a straw filled bed tic. There was no fireplace made of stone, and no walls made of splintered wood.

When Stephanie's focus became clear, tears of relief were streaming down her face. She covered her eyes in shame, mixed emotion eating at her insides.

Madge sat patiently. She comforted Stephanie with the delicate hand Stephanie had felt all her life. Stephanie stopped crying and looked into those kindly, wise old eyes. With a whimper lodged in her throat, she uttered, "I'll be fine, Madge." Using Madge's arm for support, she sat up in bed. "You can go rest now. Thank you for staying with me," she said softly.

Bewildered, Madge's brows drew together in a frown. She expected salty insults; there were none. She expected insolences and jokes; she heard neither. Madge felt Stephanie's forehead once more.

Stephanie shamefully averted her eyes and removed Madge's hand. "Really, I'll be fine. You can go now."

A look of concern enveloped Madge's face, but she left Stephanie alone, as requested.

When Madge closed the door Stephanie felt compelled to look in the mirror. She carefully swung her feet to the side of the bed and clumsily stood up. Her feet were sore and felt awkward in the plush carpet; she wriggled them slowly to get her footing. Her legs ached insistently as she gradually walked toward the mirror.

Just as Stephanie approached the mirror a ghostly reflection of the black Stephanie illuminated the mirror. A gasp escaped her lips and she jumped backwards with fright. In a flash the vaporous reflection was gone. Hesitantly, Stephanie gathered enough strength to look at her own reflection.

With nervous fingers she reached out and touched the mirror. It was cool to the touch. Stephanie tried to relax, though apprehensive about the shimmering apparition.

She noticed that she looked haggard. Using two fingers she pressed a sore area on her cheekbone. However, there was no bruise. She felt her forehead, there was no laceration. Stephanie started to run her fingers through her hair but she noticed her fingers felt taut and dry. Although, the skin on her hands felt unusual there were no burns from cooking over the open hearth. Feeling stinging sensations on her arm Stephanie rubbed her tender skin. She could almost swear she felt the irritating sting of the bushes against her skin.

Stephanie walked around her room and investigated with new eyes. High on a shelf in the corner of her room was an old framed photograph of Neal. On tip toes she reached for the photo. As she studied his smiling face, she took her fingers, kissed them then placed the kiss over the photograph. "Until now, I never realized what I did to you. I'm so sorry, Neal. I'm so sorry," she whispered tearfully, holding the photograph to her heart.

After what seemed like hours, Stephanie finally regained her sanity. She felt it was essential to have a little chat with Madge. Unlike the elders in Old Jacob's story, only Madge could solve the riddle of her turbulent dream.

Unsteadily, Stephanie's stiff legs moved slowly down the stairs. Many times she had scaled the carpeted stairs, but she never noticed how bright and elegant the red carpet was. Bending slightly, she touched the gold etching that outlined a delicate Asian design. Hanging against the wall were priceless tapestries her father purchased at auction. With wavering fingers she stroked a fine frame encasing authentic Oriental art. More artwork lined the walls as the staircase descended. Strangely, they were more striking than she remembered.

As though seeing her world for the first time, Stephanie inhaled the majesty of the living area. Placing her hands over her mouth, she gasped. "This house is awesome. I've never noticed before?"

Absently, she rubbed the treated wood of the imported banister. In a dreamlike state, Stephanie walked through the living room. She stopped to admire impressive oriental vases, prints and artwork. Her parents had surrounded her with cultural beauty all of her life. Was it her trip back in time that made her appreciate her stately surroundings? Like being in a museum, her view was breathtaking.

In awe, Stephanie sat down at the bottom of the stairs. She had to take hold of herself. Her disheveled hair was moist with perspiration. Some of it was partially pinned, while the rest lay scattered about her shoulders. Stephanie covered her face with both hands then swept the scattered mess behind her. "What a night."

The Grandfather clock chimed. Although the hollow sound was familiar, it startled her and her heart raced. Moaning, Stephanie stuck her fingers to her ears. "What a maddening sound!" At the same time, the doorbell rang. "Now what?" She noticed that her pajamas were hopelessly wrinkled. "I can't answer the door like this. "Madge," she called. Coughing and straining, Stephanie called again. "Madge! Oh, never mind. I feel so weird I don't care who sees me."

Stephanie stood up; slightly dusting off her bottom. She walked toward the door and peered into the security hole. "Pizza?" she whispered. "Madge must have ordered pizza." She slid the security lock. "Just a minute," she called. Once

Stephanie opened the door she lost her equilibrium, her world swirled out of control. Holding her spinning head she slowly walked toward the sofa.

"Are you alright?" a male voice called. Placing the pizza box on a table, he reached out to catch Stephanie. As he helped her to the sofa he inquired again. "Are you okay? Do I need to get help?" Gently, he leaned her against the sofa. "Rest here. I'll get someone."

Stephanie's hand shot up to halt his departure. "No!" she barked. "I'm okay. I was a little sick last night but I feel better now." Reaching for a tissue she blotted the cold perspiration beading on her forehead.

Looking Stephanie over, the guy knelt before her. "I don't know. You don't look so good." He felt of her forehead then looked out on the patio. "Someone is outside. Let me call her."

Stephanie grasped her throat as she swallowed. "No, please don't. I'm okay…just a little dry."

The guy sprung to his feet. "I'll get you a drink. Where's your kitchen?"

"You really don't need…"

Within seconds, the guy returned with a dainty glass of water. "Here, drink this!"

Stephanie chuckled. "You don't expect me to drink this stuff do you?"

Puzzled, the guy looked at the glass then cautiously held it at a distance. "I don't understand…"

"Hello, it comes from the tap. That stuff will kill you," she rasped. She smiled weakly and leaned back on the sofa. "Thanks anyway. There's water in the fridge."

Before Stephanie could blink the guy made a mad dash for the fridge. "Give me just a second." When he returned, he opened the bottle of water and gave it to Stephanie.

She took a swallow then placed the chilled bottle to her forehead.

"You're really good," she admitted, rubbing the bottle against her temple. "My vision went blurry for a moment. I thought I saw someone I knew."

Tugging nervously at his earlobe the guy admitted, "Well, you have seen me before."

With closed eyes, Stephanie enjoyed the coolness of the chilled bottle. "I have?"

Picking up Stephanie's chin he looked into her eyes. "Yes, you have."

Her nose was face to face with his. As the guy removed his cap Stephanie's eyes grew large, then narrowed. Her heart pounded loudly. "Zeb." She turned her face from his and scooted to the edge of the sofa. "Zeb!" she said louder.

The guy shook his head. "No, I'm not Zeb. It's me, Koda. Don't you remember? We met at the mall." He turned his face so Stephanie could get a closer look.

She put out her hand and touched his face. "Koda?" Her eyes widened. "You're Koda at the mall."

Koda cast his eyes toward the floor. "Geez, glad to see I made such an impression."

"I'm sorry, Koda. I'm so sorry. Yes, I remember you." She spoke slowly. "In such a good way — I remember you."

"Now. That's more like it. I thought I had a mug that was memorable. Most people never forget my curly red hair and green eyes." His shapely lips curled into a devious grin.

As Stephanie gathered her wits she asked, "How did you get here? I mean, did Madge call in a pizza?"

Koda shamefully averted his eyes. "You won't get ticked will you?"

Curiously, Stephanie turned her head to one side. "Why should I?"

"Well, no one really called in a pizza."

Stephanie frowned. "Really?"

Koda rubbed his chin. "There's more."

"What?"
Taking two fingers, Koda lifted his shirt. "This isn't my uniform."

"It isn't."

"No, I borrowed it from a—a friend."

Now, Stephanie was really confused. "No way!"

"Yes—way," he nodded.

"But, why Koda?" she shrugged. Koda expelled a long sigh. "Well, I guess I'd better come clean." He shrugged his shoulders. "I just wanted to see you again. I wasn't sure you'd call."

Sympathetically Stephanie cooed, "Oh, Koda. I was going to call you, but I got sick last night."

"Last night." Koda seemed surprised. "Last night. Stephanie, I met you on Friday. Today is Monday."

"It is?" Stephanie strained to look at the clock. "And, it's five in the evening!"

"Yeah—" Koda slurred, unsure of what was going on.

"You're kidding! I've been sick for days!" Stephanie arose from the sofa. "I've got to talk to, Madge."

"I'm sorry. I didn't know." Koda reached for his hat. "I guess, I'd better leave."

"No." Stephanie clasped her hand across her mouth. "I mean—give me a minute." She turned toward Koda. "I'm glad you came to see me. I mean, it's like the coolest thing ever."

Koda tossed his head to the side. "You mean you aren't ticked."

"No. Why should I get ticked? Got to see you again, didn't I?"

Koda nodded, "Yeah, but—"

"And, I've got a pizza out of the deal too, right?"

Koda stammered, "Ah, that's what I wanted to tell you."

Relieved, Stephanie smiled. "It isn't pepperoni, right?"

Stephanie's Emerald Fever

"No, it isn't pepperoni. It isn't anything." Koda's voice grew low but frank. "The box is empty."

Satisfied, Stephanie and Koda burst into laughter. "Oh! That is, like, so romantic. You went through all this trouble for me? I feel totally special."

Still fretting, Koda grinned. "I'm glad you think so. See, I've got this thing about being honest. And I..."

"What? Honest?" Hearing the word 'Honest' made Stephanie's head spin; she raised her hands to make it steady. As if there was a tremendous pounding on her head, Stephanie winced. She closed one eye then put up one finger. "Hold just a second." She calmed herself. "Don't tell me — they call you Honest Zeb, right?"

Koda frowned and shook his head. "Why would they call me that?" Abruptly, Koda stood to his feet. "I mean, if you're like, seeing this Zeb guy then—"

"Wait! Zeb! I mean, Koda! Just give me a minute, will ya? I'm like, kinda confused." She stood up and reached for Koda's arm.

Koda took a step backwards. "I don't know, Steffy. Since I've been here, all you've talked about is some guy named, Zeb. I mean, you've got to be seeing this guy."

Tightening her grip on Koda's arm Stephanie pleaded. "It's hard to explain, Koda. I'll tell you what. Give me a day or so to fully recover then we'll talk. I'm too confused right now. I was really, I mean like, putrid sick."

Calmly, Koda nodded. "I understand. I just thought you'd never call. I mean, a little insurance couldn't hurt my situation."

Stephanie's eyes sparkled. "You are so cool. Give me a few days. I'll text you when I'm better. I wouldn't want you to catch my bug or anything."

"No, dude. I don't want whatever you had. If you're better, by Friday, how about we meet at The Burger Boy?"

Stephanie brightened. "That sounds great. Wait!" Stephanie scratched her head. "Friday is my birthday. I'll be seventeen!"

"Are you sure your parents haven't made plans?"

"Nah," Stephanie shunned. "They're out of town for another week."

Koda reached out, grasped Stephanie's hand then gazed into her blue eyes. "Until Friday." He kissed her hand.

Holding her breath, Stephanie remembered her encounter with Zeb in the woods. "Until Friday."

Stephanie's Emerald Fever

Koda picked up the empty pizza box and walked toward the door. Stephanie followed. "I wish I had a magic wand to make you feel better."

"I know, right." She swept wisps of hair from her face. "I must look awful."

Koda soothed a stray strand of Stephanie's hair. "You look simply beautiful."

Stephanie smiled bashfully. "Thank you, Koda."

As Stephanie closed the door she whispered, "I thought I'd never see you again, Zeb." She inhaled and leaned against the door. Oddly her attention gravitated to Madge.

L.J. Maxie

Chapter Fifteen

When Did I Become a Witch?

We are Connected by Time and Circumstances

Chapter Fifteen

Out on the sunlit patio, Madge sat painting at an easel. She moved her brush with steady glides while Stephanie watched from the coolness of the glass French doors. When Madge was painting she always seemed contented. Feeling that someone was watching, she glanced upwards. Observing that Stephanie felt well enough to come outside, she smiled and beckoned her.

At that point, Stephanie knew her world would never be the same. Opening the French doors, she stepped into the invigorating air. Despite the busy streets below Stephanie did not feel ashamed that she was dressed in her pajamas. She had united with Zeb and all was right with the world. Making herself comfortable on an old stool, she beamed at Madge.

Madge acknowledged Stephanie with a sincere smile. "I'm painting a picture of a tree," she said cheerfully. "I've seen it in my mind a thousand times." She continued to paint, first with long strokes then with quick choppy strokes. Pointing toward the canvas with the end of her brush Madge said, "I'm going to put the faces of two girls in front of the tree, right here. One girl will be black, she will face east, the other girl will be white and she will face west. The roots of the tree will join both girls together."

Madge took a sip of her tea. "Each girl will be connected to the other by time and circumstances." She smiled softly then wiped her hands on a paint-stained cloth. "When people come into our lives we are connected by time and circumstances."

Stephanie could care less about what Madge was painting. "Time and circumstances," she repeated absently. She only wanted to be near her, to feel the reassuring warmth of her smile. After all, mother and father were always busy, but Madge was forever there for her. For sixteen years, it was Madge who took the time to listen to her problems. She had behaved badly and wished she could make up for the years of continued abuse she had inflicted upon her.

Stephanie picked up a paint brush and anxiously flicked it between her fingers. "Madge," she called quietly. "Do you still have that old bible?"

Astonished, Madge's brow made a pensive arch. "You mean the old bible that my mother gave me?"

Stephanie shyly shrugged her shoulders. "The one that was passed down through generations…the one with the dates inside."

Madge nodded. "Why? Do you need to look up a date, Honey?"

"Well, I want you to tell me about your great-great grandmother."

Madge was stunned. "My great-great grandmother. That would be Grandma Madge. What do you want to know about Grandma Madge?"

Stephanie was surprised. "Her name was Madge?"

"Yes, child. They called her 'M'dere'. I was named after her." Madge stopped painting and gave Stephanie her full attention. "What are you up to?" she asked suspiciously.

"Nothing, I swear!" Stephanie folded her arms defensively. Her blue eyes were wide with wonder yet frayed with confusion. "Can you tell me about the rest of your family?"

"Well," she continued painting. "Let's see if I remember. It's been a long time since I looked at that old thing. As far back as I can recall, my family tree started with Grandma Madge being brought from Africa."

"Africa. Wow." Stephanie placed her hand under her chin and listened.

"I'll tell you what. Why don't you just go upstairs to my room, get that old book, then we'll find out what you want to know, okay?"

"Do you think so?"

"Sure," Madge assured. "Now scoot!"

Being careful not to move too swiftly, Stephanie went upstairs. Finally arriving at Madge's room, she hesitated then placed her hand on the cold door knob. It had been years since she sought the solitude of Madge's room. Fear swelled inside her. What would she learn about herself?

Gradually, she gathered the courage to turn the lock. Once she opened the door, old memories collided with her fevered mind.

Hysterical with anticipation, Stephanie gazed around the room. She saw large framed pictures of herself as a baby, as well as pictures of her early school years. Laughing out loud, she remarked at just how fat her legs were. In some pictures she had lost her front teeth. The dresser was lined with framed birthday pictures and silly vacation pictures. "I almost forgot about those days," she said stroking the tarnished frame.

Then Stephanie realized, Madge's room was almost a private shrine of her very own life. Timidly, her hands swept over pictures drawn in childish scrawl, and she lamented. When did she stop being the perfect child, and turn into the monster no one liked?

Hand-painted Victorian lamps still adorned Madge's dressing table. After all these years they still sat on starched lace dollies. Picking up a beautiful perfume bottle, she sniffed. Her nose recalled the same powdery fragrance Madge had worn for years.

Stephanie's hands fumbled over boxes of perfume she had given Madge for Christmas. Because they were still unopened, she figured Madge never wanted to smell like bubblegum or strawberries. She always smelled the same, and always balanced decisions concerning her life.

Stephanie walked over to the Madge's bed. Recalling joyful times, she pushed against the springy softness of the plush white comforter. Sitting on the side of the bed, Stephanie mischievously bounced up and down. "Comfy, just like I remember."

Noticing a faded picture of Madge's family over the bed, Stephanie stroked the cool rails of the old iron bed. "This bed has to be over two hundred years old." An antique doll sat in the middle of Madge's bed. Stephanie toyed with the elegant green satin dress that flared around the doll's porcelain body. Running her fingers along the dolls cold lips she remembered. "I wonder why Madge never let me play with this doll. It's simply gorgeous."

The gentleness of the satin comforter entreated her to lie down. She wallowed in the comforter then curled into a ball like a purring kitten. Stretching widely, she exhaled. "Mmm."

Suddenly, her eyes fell upon the old bible sitting on the night stand. An eerie feeling wafted over her. Its black binding was old, cracked, and smelled of mold. Even so, Stephanie felt compelled to touch it. She had to know—she had to remember.

A horrible dream had transformed her life. Could this bible be a Pandora's Box of answers? Stephanie picked up the heavy bible and placed it in the middle of Madge's bed. Although she was careful, the binding started to chip into tiny flecks. Cautiously, she brushed the debris from the white comforter. "It's so fragile. I'm scared to open it."

This bible held the dates and births of the entire Andrews Family. It also held a written record of slaves who were bought and sold. Of these slaves, Madge had told her many stories. Carefully, Stephanie opened the bible. The musky vapors overcame her and she felt nauseated. "Ewww. This is, like, so disgusting. How can I go through with this?" Stephanie turned another page. She started to read. "Born this day to the Andrew's Family…"

Still reeling from her illness, Stephanie read. As her mind wandered, she nuzzled her head into Madge's pillow and her thoughts drifted. Simultaneously, she fell asleep.

Stephanie woke up to the faraway sound of Madge's voice. When she opened her eyes she felt strangely refreshed. The room appeared freshly painted. Everything seemed bright and new. Madge stood beside the bed, a long chenille robe draped around her. "What are you thinking about, Sugar?" Madge asked, sitting down on the side of the bed.

Stephanie's Emerald Fever

"I didn't break the bible. I swear! I was only looking at the pictures!"

"I know you didn't break it, Sweetie. It's a very old book." Madge lay down on the white comforter. "School starts tomorrow and you'll need your rest. Second grade is a big step. Plus, it's past your bed time."

Stephanie whined. "Not until you tell me a story." Dressed in her favorite baby doll pajamas, Stephanie scooted against Madge's body. She pulled her massive brown arm around her small frame. "You're getting heavy!" she groaned, struggling with Madge's arm.

Madge chuckled. "Silly little girl. There is no time for stories. You need your rest."

Stephanie wanted to have things her way. She flailed against Madge's motionless body. Her swift kicking exposed ringlets of baby fat around her thighs. "But, I'm too excited to sleep. Please—tell me a story about the slaves on the plantation. I want to hear a scary one."

Becoming lost in thought, Stephanie rubbed the moist brown skin on Madge's arm. Using her small fingers, she raised Madge's hand and placed her hand palm to palm. "My hands are almost as big as yours." She stretched her fingers to match the length of Madge's hand. "Will I turn brown when I get old?" she asked.

"Of course not, sweet pea. You have to be born brown."

Stephanie gazed into Madge's brown eyes. "Some of the kids at school are brown like you," she informed matter-of-factly.

"That very nice." Madge positioned a pillow beneath her head and sighed.

Stephanie squirmed as she toyed with the white ribbon on Madge's gown. "Aren't you going to put those pink curler things in your hair?"

"Yes, sweet pea. I'll do that later."

Stephanie got upon her knees. Madge knew Stephanie was headed right for her hair so she braced herself. Grasping a hand full of shiny black hair Stephanie pretended to braid Madge's hair. Finding something interesting in Madge's hair, she stopped. Selecting a few gray strands Stephanie inquired, "Why do you put these white streaks in your hair?"

Madge chuckled and smiled tenderly. "I didn't put them there, honey. God did."

"Oh," she said, examining the hair. "Will he put some in my hair?"

"Eventually," she moaned.

"Oh."

Stephanie's Emerald Fever

Making a large curl, Stephanie wrapped the shiny hair around her tiny hand. Once she felt the hair was secure she pulled her hand out. "I'm going to make a large curl." She placed the glistening curl gingerly in place. "Can I comb your hair tonight?"

"No, sugar. Not tonight."

Stephanie raised Madge's hair and whispered in her ear. "Will you give me two French braids tomorrow? I want you to part my hair down the middle, then make the braid all the way down my back, okay. Braid some ribbons into it too, okay?"

Madge's lips stretched into a quiet smile. "Okay, jewel."

"You don't French braid my hair anymore, why?"

"I don't really have time," she sighed wearily.

"Oh." Stephanie finished her elaborate hairstyle and snuggled under Madge. She wiggled her knees back and forth. "I'm wai—ting," she sang. "You didn't tell me a sto—ry."

Madge lifted Stephanie's toe and checked an old injury. "Tell you what. Why don't you tell me a story?"

"Aw—come on." Stephanie shoved Madge's body back and forth. It moved easily on the old mattress. "Remember your grandmother's porch and how she told her grandchildren stories."

"I remember."

"Well, tell me one, silly! My favorite story is the devil and the church house."

Searching her mind, Madge studied the ceiling. "Uh," she stammered, uncertain of Stephanie's claim. "I didn't tell you that story. It's too scary for little boys and girls."

"But I'm not a little girl. You told it to Daddy and he didn't get scared. Okay, I'll tell the story." Stephanie got to her knees. She projected her voice as a seasoned story teller. "Once upon a time, there was a little town in North Carlina. All of the people in this town thought they were Christians but they were serving the wrong god."

"Yes," Madge admitted, sifting her fingers through Stephanie's hair. "You do remember. What else happened?"

"Well. A scary preacher came to town riding a big fat, white horse." Stephanie swallowed. "There was a little church in North Carolina."

"Yes and…"

"It was deep in the woods. The people in the town had painted the church with white-wash paint. They made the windows pretty with stained glass windows. This church was really pretty. The seats were padded with hay and leather so the people's bottom wouldn't get sore at Sunday school."

Stephanie's eyes widened as she explained her haunting tale. Her hands gestured to demonstrate size and width. "This church had a little organ like at our church, but our organ is bigger, bigger. At night some of the people could hear the organ play."

Madge placed her hand to Stephanie's lips. "Are you sure you want to tell this story?"

"Yes, you told it to my daddy. I heard you."

"Aren't you scared?"

"No." She rolled her bright eyes towards the ceiling. "Now, let me finish." Stephanie deepened her voice to make it sound creepy. "No one in the town could play the organ, so they knew it must be some kinda magic or something.

"Now, this church had a preacher, but he was not a good man. He had sharp white teeth and a long tail like a big bad wolf. He told the people, if they wanted to go to heaven, all they had to do was bring a basket full of goodies to church and leave them at the front door."

Stephanie pretended to hold a basket. "So, once a week, the people would leave their baskets full of goodies at the church door. They had fried chicken and ice cream and pizza and yogurt in the baskets." Madge stifled her laughter by pressing her lips together. Stephanie was so absorbed, she had not noticed. "Sometime during that week all of the baskets would be gone. The people knew someone had eaten their goodies because whoever ate the food tossed the empty baskets behind the church.

"After someone gobbled up the goodies, the organ would play. This went on for years. There was a small light in the window of the church, but no one was brave enough to see who played the organ at night. I'll bet it was the Wolf Preacher. And I'll bet his tail was sticking out of his coat when he sat down to play the organ.

"One day an old Indian man came to town on a white horse. He had on a cowboy hat and a long, cowboy coat. Everyone was scared of him. He had two silver braids on each side of his head. His skin was a red color from the sun, but his eyes were as blue as mine." She held down her bottom eye lids to give Madge a better look at her eyes.

"The man never spoke to anyone. Each Sunday the old Indian man would go to the church, but after church he would go 'poof!' and disappear. One day the president said he was going to follow the old Indian man when he left the church. But, while the president was watching the old Indian man, he got up and walked right through the door without opening it! All the people got scared and called a wood cutter.

"One Sunday, the wood cutter said he would watch him until church was over. They all watched him and watched him, but when church was over, he disappeared again. But this time, the old Indian man was standing outside in front of the little church.

"He called to the wolf preacher and told him he was going to fight him for the souls of the people. Then, the two men stood in front of each other. The old Indian man grabbed the other Wolf Preacher man and lightning was flashing in their eyes.

"The sky grew dark and it started to rain, but still the two men held on to each other. All the people got scared because it was dark, but it was day. Some of them got their toys and went home. The fight went on and on.

"The Wolf Preacher man started to get weak because his word was not from the real God. All of a sudden he caught on fire and disappeared into a puff of green smoke. Some of the people were watching when that happened. After the long fight, the sun came out. The people got a broom and swept the Wolf Preacher up into a dust pan. They put him in the trash and screwed the lid on really tight.

"The old Indian man was happy. He knew the town was safe, so he got on his fat horse and rode to his castle in the woods.

"Then a fairy princess flew out of the woods and said she would be their queen if they were good. So all of the people said they would be good and she gave them back all their goodies."

Although Madge had heard many stories Stephanie had butchered, she pretended to be surprised. "Stephanie. You are a great story teller. But, are you sure the story ended like that?"

"Yes. Isn't that what you said?" she said innocently.

Madge grabbed Stephanie's cheeks and gave them a loving squeeze. "No, I did not."

Stephanie shrugged. "Well, I don't 'member what happened, exactly. I made that last part up all by myself." She smiled proudly.

Madge gave Stephanie's bottom an affectionate swat. "I'm going to count to ten and you'd better be in your bed by ten! I'll be right there in just a minute. One!"

Stephanie expelled a loud shriek and ran playfully toward the door. Her heart thumped madly as her bare feet padded swiftly down the hallway.

Overcome by excitement Stephanie awoke grinning. Stretching blissfully, she had no idea she had fallen asleep. Shaking her head in disbelief, she laughed out loud. "I can't believe I remembered that old tale." Tears started to form in her eyes as she cackled. Calming herself, she wiped her bleary eyes. "That was totally rich!" Sighing, she remembered how much Madge had meant to her. Her years had been filled with love and laughter because of Madge. How could she have damaged such wondrous and true affection?

Stephanie's Emerald Fever

Recalling the last scorching words she made to Madge, Stephanie's heart sank. As her mind rambled over the years, she recalled many harmful conversations and many years of scornful hurt. "I've been such a witch! How on earth can I make this right?"

She pulled the large bible from the bed. "Madge has been my life!" Stephanie took one last look around Madge's room then closed the door. Blinded by her own selfish behavior, she walked clumsily to the top of the stairs. Immersed in thought, she slowly descended.

Stephanie found herself standing at the patio door. Searching the evening sky, she noticed that day was slowly turning to night. How long had she slept? Sorrowfully, she opened the door. "That took a while, huh?" she said brightly, betraying her true feelings.

"Yes, it did. I wasn't worried. I figured you got caught up in some of those old photographs. You spent many hours in my room when you were a little girl. That was also your most favorite place to hide. I could always find you hiding—"

"In your closet," Stephanie finished.

Surprised, Madge acknowledged. "Yes, in my closet."

"Madge." Sincerity poured for Stephanie's lips. "Did I ever tell you that I love you?"

"Never did." Madge said winking. "But you drew me pictures that said much more."

"I'm sorry." Stephanie paused with a quiver. "I've been a real brat, huh? I don't know why people glamorize brats and being spoiled. I've had a long hard look at myself and I didn't like what I saw."

"My-my. And just who gave you this, magical mirror."

"I'm ashamed to admit it," she pointed an accusing finger at Madge. "But you did. And I need to thank you for that." She walked over to Madge and placed her cheek against her ageing gray head. "You've taught me a lot, old woman. And, I say that with honor, Madge. I say that with, like, the highest honor."

Madge smiled and looked up at Stephanie. "Who are you and what did you do with the snot-nose little brat who resides upstairs?"

Startled by Madge's frankness, Stephanie leaned back. "I deserved that, Madge. I realize what I've done—and you. How could you still love me after," she shrugged, "all I've put you through." Looking Madge right in the eyes she admitted. "There were times when I even lied on you—just to get my way with mom and dad."

"I know. Don't worry yourself about that, sweetie. I have unconditional love. It's like the same love God has for us when we do what's wrong."

"I don't understand. But I guess I will someday."

She placed the large bible on the stool. "I hope we don't get paint on it. It's very valuable you know."

"I know. You used to love looking at the pictures in that old bible. The pictures are beautiful."

"Yeah, I remember," Stephanie added stroking the old book. "Hey! Do you remember that old story about the devil and the church house?"

Stunned, Madge discharged mockingly. "Your version or mine?" They burst into laughter.

"Well, I had a little nap when I was in your room. I guess I'm still kinda tired. I wanted to know about your great-great grandmother. You know, the stuff in this bible."

"You remember a lot of stuff, Stephanie. You remembered that Grandma Madge gave birth to two daughters. Samantha and—"

"Sam! Right?"

Madge nodded. "Yes, you remembered. And her other daughter was named..."

Stephanie would not let her continue. "She was named what Madge?" Stephanie calmed herself. "I'm sorry, go on," she encouraged.

"My goodness. You woke up full of questions." She put down her brush and picked up one of a smaller size. Pondering playfully, she tapped it against her cheek. "Okay. Her name was Stephanie. They called her Miss Steffy."

"Miss Steffy!" Stephanie's eyes grew large.

Madge loaded her brush with green paint. "Back in those days it was common to call your mother 'Misses' and your father 'Mister'. Family bonds were not encouraged because a person could get sold at any time."

Stephanie sat numb, hanging on every word and fearful to tell Madge the terrifying dream. "No kidding," she said coolly.

Moving her brush cautiously, Madge revealed, "Miss Steffy delivered your great-great-great grandfather when she was only eighteen years old. Now, Old Lady Andrews almost died having that boy. Miss Steffy saved both their lives."

Stephanie gasped. "She delivered a baby? How cool is that."

Madge nodded. "Uh huh. After that, Miss Steffy was so well-loved by your family that they named their baby boy in honor

Stephanie's Emerald Fever

of her. They called him 'Stephen'. Well, after that, there was always a Stephen in your family. Because your father didn't have a son he named you Stephanie...all because of Miss Steffy."

Blinking wildly, her mouth agape, Stephanie responded. "So I am named Stephanie because of your..." She swallowed hard, shoving back her disbelief. "...your Miss Steffy?" She paused. "I'm named after *your* Miss Steffy?"

Madge nodded. "That is correct."

"Then," her chest heaved fearfully. Fighting back a wave of nausea, Stephanie held her stomach and whispered, "in my dream, I was your great-great..."

"I didn't hear you, sweetie. Are you feeling okay?" She continued with her painting. "Dream? Oh, when you're sick with a fever you dream all sorts of crazy and weird things. I assure you, it was only a dream."

Stephanie sighed, "What happened to Cassandra?"

Madge paused. She scratched her head with the end of her paint brush. "Cassandra—Cassandra. I don't think I remember any Cassandra—oh, Cassandra. Old Man Andrews' granddaughter, Cassandra?" Stephanie nodded. "Sugar, I think she died when she was about fourteen years old."

Stephanie became visibly upset. "Why Madge?"

"Honey, they said she had a bad heart. One day she just stopped breathing."

"She did not have a bad heart!" Stephanie wailed. "She was allergic to—"

"Yes? Allergic to what?" Madge's eyes narrowed as she waited for Stephanie's answer.

"Nothing," Stephanie sighed. Cassandra had reminded Stephanie of herself. Although she had not been very kind to her, she didn't deserve to die an ignorant death.

"You know what, Madge? Maybe it was a dream; maybe it was not a dream. I couldn't tell if I was living someone's life or if they were living mine. But this nightmare was, like, the grandmother of all nightmares!"

Stephanie's eyes grew large; she shuddered and shook her head in disbelief. "I will never, ever forget that dream. At times, it was a dream within a dream."

Tapping her finger against her cheek, she pondered. "I will tell my kids about my dream—no, wait!" As if inspired, she leaped to her feet and broadcasted, "I'll write a book about it! That's just what I'll do. I don't want my kids to make the same mistakes I've made."

Madge grinned doubtfully. "You're going to write a book about a bad dream? That must have been some dream."

Stephanie's Emerald Fever

Mimicking monster-like claws, Madge teased, "Do I get to hear about this scary nightmare?"

"No, Madge. You don't need to hear my nightmare. You practically lived my nightmare...every day of your life."

The End

...or is it "The Beginning"?

L.J. Maxie

Dearest Esteemed Reader,
Because you have shared in my incredible adventures, we have both been empowered with knowledge and wisdom. Slavery exists today because we are chained to old myths and ideas. To make this nation flourish, we must embrace the differences that make other cultures beautiful and unique.

Thank you,
Stephanie Denise Andrews

Stephanie's Emerald Fever

Yoruba Translation of Phrases

Ara aburo re ko i ti ya ni?........................Is your sister still sick?

Aso re lewa pupo........................Your dress is beautiful.

Beni. O je osan ti ko i kpon..................Yes, she ate green plums.

(The O sound in osan is pronounced aw.)

Ko gbadun..She is silly

Kpele. She ara le?................................Hi. How are you?

Mo gbadun Orin Yen..I like the music

O'yato................................... ....She seems strange.
(The O sound in yato is pronounced aw.)

Dr. Aworuwa Bosede, Translator for Yoruba Phrases.
(October, 2006)

Stephanie's Emerald Fever

About The Author

Mrs. Maxie is the author of the time travel novel, Stephanie's Emerald Fever. She resides in the North East Texas area with her loving husband. Maxie has a degree in Behavioral Sciences as well as a Masters degree in Education. She is a public speaker, youth counselor, and an activist for 'Prevention of Family Violence.

During the early 90's Stephanie's Emerald Fever was a nagging thought in my head. To release the pressure, I wrote the title as a screen play. Later, I was given the opportunity to bring this book to life in print, then on the stage. It was quite an exhilarating experience! I would like to thank the actors who gave up their lives for that powerful production.

Contact: L.J. Maxie
maxie1661@aol.com
http://ljmaxie.webs.com

Join Me! Check out my website. Catch up on the latest book signings and speaking engagements!

www.ingramcontent.com/pod-product-compliance
Lightning Source LLC
Chambersburg PA
CBHW022356040426
42450CB00005B/200